P9-CAM-754

Claude Lévi-Strauss
AN INTRODUCTION

OCTAVIO PAZ

Claude Lévi-Strauss
AN INTRODUCTION

Translated from the Spanish by
J. S. BERNSTEIN and
MAXINE BERNSTEIN

Cornell University Press
ITHACA AND LONDON

First published 1970

Translated from *Claude Lévi-Strauss o el nuevo festín de Esopo* (1st ed.; México, D.F.: Joaquín Mortiz, 1967)

International Standard Book Number 0-8014-0576-9
Library of Congress Catalog Card Number 73-121571

PRINTED IN THE UNITED STATES OF AMERICA
BY VAIL-BALLOU PRESS, INC.

Contents

Claude Lévi-Strauss
AN INTRODUCTION

I

A geological metaphor. Verbal union and sexual union: values, signs, women.

Some fifteen years ago, a commentary by Georges Bataille on *Les Structures élémentaires de la parenté* revealed Claude Lévi-Strauss's existence to me. I bought the book and after several unfruitful attempts to read it, I put it down. My good will as an amateur anthropologist and my interest in the theme (the incest taboo) came to grief when faced with the technical nature of the book. Last year, an article in *The Times Literary Supplement* (London) reawakened my curiosity. I read *Tristes Tropiques* voraciously and then, immediately after, and with growing astonishment, *Anthropologie structurale*, *La Pensée sauvage*, *Le Totémisme aujourd'hui*, and *Le Cru et le cuit*. The last is a particularly difficult book and the reader suffers a kind of intellectual vertigo in following the author in his winding path through the underbrush of Bororo and Ge Indian myths. To survey this labyrinth is laborious but fascinating: many sections of this "concerto" of understanding elated me; others enlightened, and still others annoyed me. Although I read for pleasure and without taking notes, the reading of Lévi-Strauss revealed so much to me and awakened so many questions in me that, almost without realizing it, I made some notes. This book is the result of my reading. It is a resumé of my impressions and reflections, and has no critical pretensions whatever.

The writings of Lévi-Strauss have a threefold importance: anthropological, philosophical, and esthetic. It is scarcely necessary in respect to the first to say that specialists consider his works on kinship, myths, and primitive thought to be fundamental. American ethnography and ethnology are indebted to him for remarkable research; moreover, in almost all his works there are many scattered observations on problems of prehistory and the history of our continent: the antiquity of man in the New World, the relations between Asia and America, art, cooking, Indo-American myths. . . . Lévi-Strauss distrusts philosophy, but his books comprise a permanent dialogue, nearly always a critical one, with philosophical thought and especially with phenomenology. On the other hand, his conception of anthropology as a part of some future semiology or general theory of signs, and his reflections on thought (primitive and civilized) are, in a certain sense, a philosophy: his central theme is the place of man in the natural system. In a narrower though no less stimulating sense, his work as a "moralist" also has philosophical interest: Lévi-Strauss continues the tradition of Rousseau and Diderot, Montaigne and Montesquieu. His meditation on non-European societies produces a critique of Western institutions, and this reflection culminates, in the last part of *Tristes Tropiques*, in a curious profession of faith, now quite frankly philosophical, in which he offers the reader a sort of synthesis of the responsibilities of the anthropologist, Marxist thought, and the Buddhist tradition. Among Lévi-Strauss's contributions to esthetics I will mention two studies on Indo-American art—one dealing with representational dualism in Asia and America, the other on the theme of the serpent whose body is full of fish—and his brilliant, although not always convincing, ideas on music, art, and poetry. I will say little about the esthetic value of his work. His prose makes me think of that of three authors, who are not perhaps his favorites: Bergson, Proust, and Breton. In them, as in Lévi-Strauss, the reader is confronted by a language which is constantly shifting between the concrete and the abstract, between direct intuition of the object and analysis: a thought which sees ideas as perceptible forms and sees forms as intellectual signs. . . . The first thing which is surprising is the variety in a work which claims to be only anthropological; the

5

second surprise is the unity of thought. This unity is not the unity of science, but rather of philosophy, even though it is an antiphilosophical philosophy.

Lévi-Strauss has on various occasions alluded to the influences which determined the direction of his thinking: geology, Marxism, and Freud. A landscape is seen as a puzzle: hills, boulders, valleys, trees, ravines. This disorder has a hidden meaning; it is not a juxtaposition of different forms, but rather the coming together in one place of distinct space-times: the geological eras. Just as is language, landscape is diachronic and synchronic at the same time: it is the condensed history of the ages of the Earth and it is also a nexus of relationships. A cross-section shows that what is hidden, the invisible strata, is a "structure" which determines and gives meaning to the strata which lie above it. To his intuitive discovery of geology were later joined the lessons of Marxism (a geology of society), and psychoanalysis (a geology of the psyche). This triple lesson can be summed up in a phrase: Marx, Freud, and geology taught him to explain the visible by the hidden; that is: to search out the relationship between the sensible and the rational. Not a dissolution of reason in the unconscious, but a search for the rationality of the unconscious: a superrationalism. To continue the metaphor, these influences establish the geology of his thought: they are determinants in a general sense. No less decisive for its formation were the sociological work of Marcel Mauss and structural linguistics.

I've already said that my comments are not strictly scientific in nature; I examine Lévi-Strauss's ideas with the curiosity, passion, and concern of a reader who wants to understand them because he knows that, like all of science's great hypotheses, they are destined to change our image of the world and of man. Thus, I do not intend to place his thought in the modern trends of anthropology, although it is apparent that that thought is part of a scientific tradition, no matter how original it seems to us and may in fact be. Lévi-Strauss himself, furthermore, in his *Leçon inaugurale* at the Collège de France (January, 1960) has made known his debt to Anglo-American anthropology and to French sociology. Even more explicitly, in several chapters of *Anthropologie structurale*, and in many places in *Le Totémisme aujourd'hui*, he reveals and clarifies his agreements and disagreements with Boas, Malinowski, and Radcliffe-Brown. On this point, it is worth emphasizing that again and again he has recalled that his first works were conceived and elaborated in close connection with Anglo-American anthropology. Still, it was the ideas of Mauss which prepared him for the lesson of structural linguistics, and to leap, more totally than other anthropologists, from functionalism to structuralism. Durkheim had asserted that juridical, economic, artistic, or religious phenomena were "projections of society"; the whole explained the parts. Mauss accepted this idea but pointed out that each phenomenon has its own characteristics and that Durkheim's "total social fact" was made up of a series of superimposed planes: each phenomenon, without losing its uniqueness, alludes to the other phenomena. For this reason, what matters is not the global explanation, but the relation between the phenomena: society is a totality because it is a system of relationships. The social totality is neither substance nor concept, but rather "consists, ultimately, of the gamut of relationships between all the planes."

In his famous essay on the gift, Mauss points out that the gift is reciprocal and circular: things which are exchanged are at the same time total facts; or in other words: things (tools, products, wealth) are the vehicles for relationships. They are values and they are signs. The institution of *potlach*—or any other analogous one—is a system of relationships: the reciprocal giving assures, or rather, realizes the relationship. Thus, a society's culture is not the sum of its tools and artifacts; society is a total system of relationships which encompasses the material as well as the juridical, religious, and artistic aspects. Lévi-Strauss takes up Mauss's lesson, and taking linguistics as an example, conceives of society as an aggregate of signs: a structure. Thus he moves from the idea of society as a totality of functions to the idea of a system of communications. It is revealing that Georges Bataille (*La Part maudite*) has arrived at different conclusions from Mauss's essay. For Bataille, it is a question not so much of reciprocity, circulation, and communication as of collision and violence, power over others and self-destruction: the *potlach* is an activity analogous to eroticism and to play; its essence is no different from that of sacrifice. Bataille tries to decipher the historical and psychological content of the *potlach*; Lévi-Strauss considers it to be an atemporal structure, independent of its content. His position brings him face to face with the functionalism of Anglo-Saxon anthropology, historicism, and phenomenology.

Below I shall deal in more detail with the theme of the polemical relation between Lévi-Strauss's thought and historicism and phenomenology. At this point, it is apropos summarily to sketch his affinities and differences with the points of view of Malinowski and Radcliffe-Brown. For the former, "social facts cannot be reduced to scattered fragments; man lives them, car-

9

ries them out, and this subjective consciousness is as much a form of reality as is their objective condition." Malinowski's great merit lay in having shown *experimentally* that the ideas which a society has of itself are an inseparable part of that society; in this way, he reevaluated the notion of the meaning of the social fact; but he reduced the significance of social phenomena to the category of function. The idea of relationship which is central in Mauss is resolved in the idea of function: things and institutions are signs for functions. For his part, Radcliffe-Brown introduced the notion of structure into the field of anthropology, except that the great English scientist thought that "structure is the order of facts: something given in the observation of each particular society. . . ." Lévi-Strauss's originality rests on his seeing the structure not solely as a phenomenon resulting from the association of men but as "a system ruled by an internal cohesion—and this cohesion, which is inaccessible to the observer of an isolated system, is revealed in the study of the transformations by means of which similar properties are rediscovered in systems which are apparently different" (*Leçon inaugurale*). Each system—kinship patterns, mythologies, classifications, etc.—is like a language which can be translated into the language of another system. For Radcliffe-Brown, structure "is the lasting way which groups and individuals have of constituting themselves and associating themselves within a society"; therefore, each structure is particular to itself and untranslatable to others. Lévi-Strauss thinks that structure is a system, and that each system is ruled by a code which—if the anthropologist succeeds in deciphering it—permits its translation into another system. Finally, in contrast to Malinowski and Radcliffe-Brown, Lévi-Strauss sees unconscious categories, far from being irrational or merely functional, as having so to speak an immanent rationality. The code is unconscious—and rational. Consequently, nothing is more natural than his seeing in the phonological system of structural linguistics the most comprehensive, transparent, and universal model of that unconscious reason which underlies all social phenomena, whether we are dealing with kinship systems or mythological inventions. He was certainly not the first to think of linguistics as the model for anthropological research. But whereas Anglo-American anthropologists considered it a branch of anthropology, Lévi-Strauss maintains that anthropology is (or will be) a branch of linguistics. That is: a part of a future general science of signs.

At the risk of repeating what others have often said (and said better than I), I must pause and clarify a little the particular relation which connects Lévi-Strauss's thought with linguistics.[1] As is well known, the transition from functionalism to structuralism takes place in linguistics between 1920 and 1930. Upon the idea that "each item of language—sentence, word, morpheme, phoneme, etc.—exists solely to fulfill a function, generally a communicative one" another is superimposed: "No element of language can be evaluated if it is not considered in relationship with the other elements." * The notion of relation becomes the foundation of the theory: language is a system of relations. For his part, Ferdinand de Saussure had made a crucial distinction: the dual character of the sign, made up of a *signifier* and a *signified*, sound and sense. This relation—although not entirely explained —defines the field proper to linguistics: each of the elements of language, including the smallest ones "has two aspects, one the signifier and the other the signified." Analysis must keep this duality in mind and proceed from the text to the sentence, and from there to the word and to the morpheme, the minimal unit which has meaning. Research does not stop at the lat-

* Josef Vachek, *The Linguistic School of Prague*, 1966. [Tr. note: A *Prague School Reader in Linguistics* (Bloomington: Indiana University Press, 1964). In footnotes, all bracketed material has been supplied by the translators.]

ter because the founding of phonology allowed another decisive step to be taken: the analysis of phonemes, units which "despite their not having a
meaning of their own, participate in the significance."
The signifying function of the phoneme consists in its
designating a relationship of alteration or opposition
to other phonemes; even though the phoneme lacks
meaning, its position within the word and its relation
with the other phonemes makes meaning possible.
The whole edifice of language rests on this binary opposition. Phonemes can be broken down into smaller
elements, which Jakobson calls "bundles or groups of
differential particles." * Like atoms and their particles,
the phoneme is a "relational field": a structure. That
is not all: phonology shows that linguistic phenomena
obey an unconscious structure: we speak without
knowing that, each time we do, we are setting a phonological structure in motion. Thus, speech is a mental
and physiological operation which rests on strict laws
which, nonetheless, elude the mastery of clear consciousness.

The analogies between linguistics and physics, genetics, and information theory on the one hand, and

* Roman Jakobson, *Essais de linguistique générale* [tr. de
l'anglais par Nicolas Ruwet], Paris [Editions de Minuit],
1963.

"the psychology of form" on the other, come readily to mind. Lévi-Strauss set about applying the structural method of linguistics to anthropology. Nothing is more justified: language is not only a social phenomenon, which constitutes at the same time the foundation of every society and man's most perfect social expression. The privileged place of language turns it into a model for anthropological research: "Like phonemes, kinship terms are elements of meaning; like them, they do not acquire this meaning except as a condition of their taking part in a system; like phonemic systems, kinship systems are spiritual elaborations at the level of unconscious thought; lastly, the recurrence of kinship patterns and marriage rules in widely separated regions and among profoundly different peoples, makes us think that, as in the case of phonology, the visible phenomena are the product of the interplay of hidden general laws. . . . In a *different order of reality*, kinship phenomena are phenomena of the *same type* as linguistic ones." * It is not a question, naturally, of *transferring* linguistic analysis into anthropology, but of *translating* it into anthropological terms. Among the forms of translation there is one that Jakobson calls "transmutation": the interpretation of linguistic signs by means of a system

* Claude Lévi-Strauss, *Anthropologie structurale*.

of nonlinguistic signs. In this case the operation consists, on the contrary, of the interpretation of a system of nonlinguistic signs (for example: kinship rules) by means of linguistic signs.

I will not describe at length the always rigorous and at times daringly ingenious form which Lévi-Strauss's interpretation takes. I will only point out that his method is based more on an analogy than on an identity. Moreover, I will offer this observation: if language—and with it all society: ritual, art, economics, religion—is a sign system, what do the signs mean? An author whom Jakobson cites frequently, the philosopher Charles Peirce, says: "The sense of a symbol is its translation into another symbol." In a manner contrary to Husserl's, the Anglo-American philosopher reduces the meaning to an operation: a sign refers us to another sign. A circular answer, and one which cancels itself out: if language is a system of signs, a sign of signs, *what does this sign of signs signify?* Linguists concur with mathematical logic, though for opposite reasons, in their horror of semantics. Jakobson is aware of this failing: "After having annexed the sounds of the word to linguistics, and founded phonology, we ought now to incorporate linguistic meanings into the science of language." So be it. Meanwhile, I observe that this concept of language ends in a dilemma: if only language has meaning, the nonlinguistic universe is lacking in meaning and even in reality; or, everything is language, from the atoms and their particles to the stars. Neither Peirce nor linguistics gives us the tools to affirm either the former or the latter. A triple omission: to begin with, the problem of the connection between sound and sense, which is not simply the effect of an arbitrary convention as F. de Saussure thought, is side-stepped; then, the theme of the relationship between nonlinguistic reality and meaning, between being and meaning, is excluded; and lastly, the main question is omitted: the meaning of meaning. I am aware that this criticism is not entirely applicable to Lévi-Strauss. He is more daring than the linguists and the proponents of symbolic logic; the constant theme of his meditations is precisely that of the relations between the universe of discourse and nonverbal reality, thought and things, meaning and nonmeaning.

In his studies of kinship, Lévi-Strauss proceeds in a manner contrary to most of his predecessors: he does not try to explain the incest taboo on the basis of marriage rules, but rather he uses the former to make the latter intelligible. The universality of the taboo, no matter what variations it adopts in one or another human group, is analogous to the universality of language, again whatever the characteristics and diversity of tongues and dialects. Another analogy: it is a taboo which does not occur in the animal kingdom—by which it can be inferred that it does not have a biological or instinctual origin—and which, nonetheless, is a complex unconscious structure, like language. Finally, all societies know and practice it, but until now—despite the abundance of mythical, religious, and philosophical interpretations—we have not had a rational theory which explains its origin and effectiveness. Lévi-Strauss properly rejects all the hypotheses with which people have tried to explain the enigma of the incest taboo, from the teleological and eugenic ones to that of Freud. In referring to Freud, he indicates that to attribute the origin of the prohibition to the son's desire for the mother and murder of the father, is a hypothesis which reveals the obsessions of modern man, but which does not correspond to any historical or anthropological reality. It is a "symbolic dream": it is not the origin but the consequence of the prohibition.

The taboo is not purely negative; it does not tend to suppress unions but rather to differentiate them: this union is not permissible and that one is. The rule is made up of a *yes* and a *no*, a binary opposition similar

to that of elementary linguistic structures. It is a
model which directs and distributes the flow of generations. It thus fulfills a distinguishing and mediating
function—differentiating, selecting, and combining—
which turns sexual unions into a system of meanings.
It is a scheme "by which and in which the transition
from nature to culture is fulfilled." The metamorphosis of raw sound into a phoneme is reproduced in the
transformation of animal sexuality into a matrimonial
system; in both cases the change is due to a dual operation (this *no*, that *yes*) which selects and combines
—verbal signs or women. In the same way that natural
sounds reappear in articulate speech, but now en-
dowed with meaning, the biological family reappears
in human society, but now changed. The "atom" or
minimal kinship element is not the biological or natural one—father, mother, and son—but rather is made
up of four terms: brother and sister, father and daughter. It is impossible to follow Lévi-Strauss through his
whole exploration, and that is why I limit myself to
quoting one of his conclusions: "The primitive and ir-
reducible character of the kinship unit is a consequence of the incest taboo. . . . In human society a
man cannot get a woman except from another man,
who entrusts him with his daughter or his sister." The
taboo has no other object than to permit the circula-

tion of women, and in this sense, it is a counterpart of the obligation to give, as studied by Mauss.

The taboo is reciprocal and because of it communication is established between men: "The matrimonial rules and kinship systems are a sort of language"—a group of operations which transmit messages. To the objection that women are values and not signs, and words signs and not values, Lévi-Strauss replies that no doubt originally the latter were also values (a hypothesis which does not seem wrongheaded to me if we think of the *energy* which certain words still radiate); regarding women: they were (and are) signs, elements of that system of meanings which is the kinship system. . . . I am not an anthropologist and ought to keep my peace. I will dare to offer at any rate a humble comment: the hypothesis explains with great elegance and precision the rules of kinship and matrimony by the universal taboo against incest, but how are the taboo itself, its origin, and its universality, explained? I confess that it is difficult for me to accept the idea that an inflexible norm, and one in which it is proper to see the source of all morality—it was the first "No" which set man against nature—is simply a rule for transfer, a device destined to facilitate the exchange of women. Furthermore, I miss any description of the phenomenon; Lévi-Strauss describes for us the operation of the rules, not the thing they regulate: attraction for and repulsion by the opposite sex, the view of the body as a node of beneficent or noxious forces, rivalries and friendships, economic and religious considerations, the fear and desire which a woman or man from a different social group or another race awakens, the family and love, the violent and complicated interplay between veneration and defilement, fear and desire, aggression and transgression —all that magnetic sphere, magic and eroticism, which the word incest covers. What is meant by this taboo, which nothing and no one explains and which, although it seems to have no biological justification or *raison d'être*, is the root of all prohibition? What is the basis of this universal *No*? It is true that this *No* contains a *Yes*: the taboo not only separates animal from social sexuality, but also, that *Yes* establishes and constitutes society as does language. The incest taboo confronts us, on another level, with the same enigma as does language: if language creates us, gives us meaning, what is the meaning of that meaning? Language gives us the means of *speech*, but what does speech *mean*? The question about incest is similar to the one about the meaning of meaning. Lévi-Strauss's reply is a singular one: we are confronting an unconscious operation of the human spirit which, in itself, lacks any meaning or foundation, although it does not lack usefulness: thanks to it—and to language, work, and myth—men are men. The question about the foundation of the incest taboo is resolved in the question about the meaning of man; and this one is resolved in the one about the spirit. Thus, one must enter into a sphere in which the spirit works with greater freedom since it confronts neither economic process nor sexual reality, but only itself.

II

Symbols, metaphors, and equations. Position and meaning. Asia, America, and Europe. Three transparencies: the rainbow, poison, and the weasel. The spirit: something which is nothing.

Lévi-Strauss takes a position on myth which is frankly intellectual, and he laments the modern predilection for attributing powers to affective life which it does not have: "It is a mistake to think that clear ideas can be born out of confused emotions." * He also criticizes the phenomenology of religion which tries to reduce to "unformed and ineffable feelings" intellectual phenomena which are only apparently different from those of our logic. The supposed opposition between logical thought and mythical thought reveals only our own ignorance: we know how to read a treatise of philosophy but we do not know how myths should be read. Certainly, we have a key, the words of which they are made up, but their meaning escapes us because language in myths occupies a place similar to the place the phonemic system occupies within language itself. Lévi-Strauss begins his argument with this idea: the plurality of myths, in all times and all

* A. M. Hocart, cited by Lévi-Strauss in *La Structure des mythes.*

places, is no less notable than the repetition of certain processes in all mythic accounts. The same thing occurs in the universe of language: the plurality of texts is a result of the combination of a very small number of fixed linguistic elements. Likewise, mythical elaboration does not obey laws different from linguistic laws: selection and combination of verbal signs. The distinction between language and speaking, proposed by F. de Saussure, is also applicable to myths. The former is synchronic and assumes a reversible time; the latter is diachronic and its time is irreversible. Or as we say in English: "It's said and done." * Myth is speech, its time refers to what happened and it is an unrepeatable utterance; at the same time, it is language: a structure which is actualized each time we tell the story again.

The comparison between myth and language leads Lévi-Strauss to search out the constituent elements of the former. Those elements cannot be phonemes, morphemes, or "semantemes," for if they were, myth would be a language like other ones. The constituent units of myth are phrases or minimal sentences which, because of their position in the context, describe an important relationship between the different aspects,

* Tr. note: Paz's example in Spanish, "Lo dicho, dicho está," means literally "What's said is said."

incidents, and characters of the tale. Lévi-Strauss suggests that we call these units *mythemes*. Since a myth is a story told with words, how can we distinguish the mythemes from other, purely linguistic, units? Mythemes are "nodes or bundles of mythical relationships" and they operate on a level above the purely linguistic. The phonemic structure is found on the lowest level; on the second one, syntactic structure, common to all discourse; on the third, mythical language proper. Syntactic structure is to the mythical structure as phonemic structure is to the syntactic. If research succeeds in isolating mythemes, as phonology did with phonemes, we will be able to make use of a group of relationships which constitute a structure. The combinations of mythemes ought to produce myths as inexorably and regularly as phonemes produce syllables, morphemes, words, and texts. The mythemes are at once signifying (with the tale) and presignifying (as elements of a second discourse: the myth). Thanks to mythemes, myths are speaking and language, irreversible time (tale) and reversible time (structure), diachrony and synchrony. Again, in advance of offering my point of view more completely at the end of this essay, I will offer this reflection: if myth is a para-language, its relation with language is opposite to the relation of a kinship system with lan-

27

guage. The latter is a system of significances which makes use of nonlinguistic elements; myth operates with language as if the latter were a presignifying system: what the myth says is *not* what the words of the myth say. The kinship system is deciphered by means of a superordinate key: language; what might the para-linguistic key be which could decipher the meaning of myths? And that key, would it be translatable into language's key? In sum, myths make us confront once again the problem of the meaning of meaning.

In his essay *La Structure des mythes,* a prelude to other more ambitious works, Lévi-Strauss uses the story of Oedipus as the starting point for his ideas. He is not interested in the content of the myth, nor does he try to offer a new interpretation; but he attempts to decipher its structure: the relational system which determines it and which is probably no different from the one in all other myths. He is seeking a general, formal, and combinatorial law. Not without raising the eyebrows of more than one anthropologist and many Hellenists and psychologists, he collected the greatest possible number of versions and then he isolated the minimal units, the mythemes, which appear in these variant readings. Some have criticized this procedure: how can mythemes be determined objectively? The objection is without foundation if we remember that one of the characteristics of myths is the recurrence of certain themes and motifs. In this way, we can even reconstruct incomplete versions and even discover mythemes which, for one or another reason, do not appear in any version. Such is the case with the bodily defect of Oedipus, which does not figure in the known variants. Once he determined the mythemes Lévi-Strauss wrote them on a card, arranged in horizontal and vertical columns. Each mytheme designated a bundle of relations; that is, it was the concrete expression of a relational function. Here, in very simplified form, is Lévi-Strauss's chart:

1	2	3	4
	Oedipus kills Laius, his father		
		Oedipus immolates the Sphinx	Oedipus: swollen feet
Oedipus marries his mother			
	Eteocles kills his brother		
Antigone buries her brother			

If we read from right to left, *we are telling* the
myth; if we read downward, we enter into its structure. The first column corresponds to the idea of kinship relations which are too intimate (between Oedipus and his mother, Antigone and her brother); the
second describes a devaluation of these same relations
(Oedipus kills his father, Eteocles his brother); the
third refers to the destruction of monsters; the fourth
to an impediment in walking. The relation between
the first and second column is obvious: they are con-
nected by a double and contrary excess, exaggerating
or minimizing kinship relations. The relationship between Oedipus and the Sphinx is reproduced in that
of Cadmus and the dragon; to found Thebes the hero
must kill the monster. It is a relationship between man
and the earth which alludes to the conflict between
belief in the earthly origin of our species (autochthony) and the fact that each one of us is the child
of a man and a woman. As a result, the third column
is a negation of this relationship and reproduces, on
another level, the theme of the second column. Many
myths show us men born of the earth as invalids,
lame, or of halting gait. Although its meaning is not
clear, analysis confirms that Oedipus's name, like the
names of his father and his grandfather (the former

was lame, the latter deaf), refers to a bodily defect.*
Therefore, the fourth column affirms what the third
denies and, again on another level, repeats the theme
of the first. Thus, the relation between the third column and the fourth is of the same order as that between the first and second. We face a double pair of
opposites: the first is to the second as the third is to
the fourth. The formula can be varied: the first is
homologous with the fourth, and the second with the
third. In moral terms: the parricide is atoned for by
incest; in cosmological terms: to deny autochthony
(to be a *complete* man) implies killing the monster of
the earth. The defect is atoned for by excess. The
myth offers a solution to the conflict by means of a
system of symbols which operate as do logical and
mathematical systems.

When he finds the structure of the myth of Oedipus, Lévi-Strauss is in a position to apply the same
combinatorial laws to myths of other civilizations.

* Does Oedipus's name mean "swollen foot" or "the one
who knows the answer to the riddle of the feet"? As is well
known, the Sphinx asks: What animal has four feet at morn-
ing, two at noon, and three at dusk? The answer is: man. It
seems to me that the riddle of the Sphinx confirms Lévi-
Strauss's hypothesis: the theme of columns three and four is
the theme of man's origin.

Boas had pointed out that riddles as a genre are almost completely missing among North American Indians. There are two exceptions: the ceremonial buffoons or clowns of the Pueblo—according to the myths a product of incestuous sexual union—who amuse spectators with riddles; and certain myths of the Algonquian Indians which relate to owls who propose riddles which, on pain of death, the hero must resolve. The analogy with the Oedipus myth is a double one: on the one hand, between incest and riddles; on the other, between the Sphinx and owls. Thus there is a relationship between incest and a riddle: the answer to a riddle unites two irreconcilable terms and incest two irreconcilable people. The mental operation in the two cases is identical: uniting two contradictory terms. This relationship is reproduced in other myths, only in opposite fashion. For example, in the Grail myth. In Oedipus a monster posits a question without an answer. Actually, Percivale does not dare to ask what the magical vessel is and what it is for. In one case, the myth presents a character who abuses illicit sexual union and who, at the same time, has such subtlety of mind that he can resolve the riddle of the Sphinx; in the other, there is a chaste and shy character who does not dare formulate the question which will dispel the charm. Illicit sexual union = resolution of a riddle which postulates the union of two contradictory terms; sexual abstinence = inability to ask. The conflict between autochthony and the real, sexual origin of man demands an opposite solution. The existence of the Sphinx (autochthony) implies the devaluation of consanguinous ties (parricide); the disappearance of the monster, the exaggeration of those same ties (incest). Although Lévi-Strauss refrains from studying the myths of historical civilizations (the Oedipus myth is more an illustration of his ideas than a study in Greek mythology), I note that the same logic is at work in the myth of Quetzalcóatl. Several researchers have devoted notable studies to the topic and it is hardly necessary to recall, for example, the brilliant interpretation of Laurette Sejourné. Yet, Lévi-Strauss's method offers the possibility of studying myth more as a mental operation than as a historical projection. The historical elements do not disappear but they are integrated into that system of transformations which embraces kinship systems and political institutions as well as mythology and ritual practices. I am aware that structuralism does not try to explain history: the event, the occurrence, is a domain which it does not deal with; but then, from the point of view of anthropology, as Lévi-Strauss conceives it, history is but one of the variants of the structure. The myth of

Quetzalcóatl is a historical product—whether or not its main character was historical—to the degree to which it is a religious creation of a specific society; at the same time, it is a mental operation subject to the same logic as other myths—without excluding modern myths, such as the myth of the Revolution. Here I will limit myself to pointing out certain traits and significant elements: Tezcatlipoca, lame god and lord of magicians and sorcerers, intimately associated with the myth of human sacrifices, tempts Quetzalcóatl and leads him to commit the double sin of adultery and incest (Quetzalcóatl gets drunk and lies with his sister). Contrary to what happens with Oedipus, savior of Thebes when he deciphers the riddle of the Sphinx, Quetzalcóatl is a victim of the sorcerer's deceit and he thus loses his kingdom and brings about the loss of Tula. The Aztecs, who always considered themselves the heirs of the grandeur of Tula, were *performing* again the myth of Quetzalcóatl (I mean, they were celebrating it, living it) at the moment of the Spanish conquest, but only in reverse. Perhaps the myth of Quetzalcóatl, if we succeeded in deciphering its structure, might give us the key to the two mysteries of the ancient history of Mexico: the end of the great theocracies and the beginning of historical cultures (the opposition between Teotihuacan and Tula, one might say, to simplify matters) and the attitude of the Aztecs toward Cortez.

In the second part of his essay Lévi-Strauss draws on several Pueblo Indian myths to broaden his argument. An opposition of irreconcilable terms is also manifested in them: autochthony and biological birth, change and permanence, life and death, agriculture and hunting, peace and war. These oppositions are not always evident because at times the original terms have been replaced by others. The permutation of one term by another has as its object the finding of mediating terms between the opposites. Mythical thinking does not operate differently from our logic; it differs in its use of symbols because in the place of propositions, axioms, and abstract signs it makes use of heroes, gods, animals, and other elements of the natural and cultural world. It is a concrete logic and no less rigorous than the logic of mathematicians. The position of the mediating terms is privileged. For example, change implies death for the Pueblo Indians; by the intervention of the mediator, *agriculture*, it is transformed into vital growth. War, a synonym of death, is transformed into life by another mediation: *hunting*. The opposition between carnivorous and herbivorous animals is resolved in another mediation: coyotes and buzzards who feed on flesh like carnivores,

35

but who, like herbivores, are not hunters. The same operation of permutation rules the careers of gods and heroes. A mediator corresponds to each opposition, so that the function of Messiahs is clarified: they are incarnations of logical propositions which resolve a contradiction. Something similar occurs with divine twins, hermaphrodite gods, and a curious character, the mythical trickster who appears in many myths and rites. Psychological acuity is no less, in this case, than logical rigor: laughter, as is well known, dissolves a contradiction into a convulsive unity, one which denies both terms of the opposition. Among mythical tricksters there is one, the *Ash boy*, who occupies in Pueblo mythology a place similar to that of Cinderella in the West: both are mediators between darkness and light, ugliness and beauty, wealth and poverty, the lower and the upper classes. The relationship between Cinderella and the *Ash boy* takes on the form of a symmetrical reversal. Below, we shall find this relationship again, between certain European myths and legends and others from America.[2]

The ambiguity of the mediator is explained not so much by psychological reasons as it is by its position in the middle of the formula: it is a term which permits the opposition to be dissolved or transcended. For this reason, a positive term (god, hero, monster, animal, plant, star) can be transformed into a negative one: its qualities depend on its position within the myth. No element has a meaning of its own; the meaning springs from the context: Oedipus is "good" when he immolates the Sphinx, "bad" when he marries his mother; he is "weak" when he limps, "strong" when he kills his father. Each term can be replaced by another, provided that there is a necessary relationship between them. Myths obey the same laws as symbolic logic; if proper names and mythemes are replaced by mathematical signs, the myth and its variants—even the most contradictory ones—can be condensed into a formula. . . . At the end of his study, Lévi-Strauss asserts that myth "has for its object the offering of a logical model to resolve a contradiction—something which cannot be done if the contradiction is real." I note, as a result, a difference between mythical thought and the thought of modern man: in myth a logic unfolds which does not confront reality and its coherence is merely formal; in science, the theory must be subjected to the proof of experiment; in philosophy, thought is critical. I admit that myth is logical, but I do not see how it can be knowledge. Lastly, Lévi-Strauss's method forbids an analysis of the particular meaning of myths: on the one hand, he thinks these meanings contradictory, arbitrary, and to a cer-

37

tain extent insignificant; on the other, he asserts that the meaning of myths unfolds in a realm beyond that of language. The system of symbolization reproduces itself endlessly. Myth engenders myths: oppositions, permutations, mediations, and new oppositions. Each solution is "slightly different" from the one before, so that the myth "grows like a spiral": the new version modifies it, and at the same time, repeats it. Therefore, Freud's interpretation, its psychological value apart, is one more version of the Oedipus myth. One could add that Lévi-Strauss's study constitutes yet another version, no longer in psychological terms but in terms of linguistics and symbolic logic. This is the theme, precisely, of *Le Cru et le cuit*. An analysis of nearly two hundred South American myths, it works like a transformational device which encompasses and "translates" them into intellectual terms. This translation is a transmutation, and that is why, as the author tells us, it is "a myth of American myths." To a certain extent, *Le Cru et le cuit* answers my question about the meaning of myths: as with the symbols of Peirce, the meaning of one myth is another myth. Each myth reveals its meaning in another one, which, in its turn, refers to another, and so on in succession to the point where all these allusions and meanings weave a text: a group or family of myths. This text alludes to another and another; the texts compose a whole, not so much a discourse as a system in motion and perpetual metamorphosis: a language. The mythology of the American Indians is a system, and that system is a language. The same may be said of Indo-European and Mongolian mythology: each one constitutes a language. On the other hand, the meaning of a myth depends on its position in the group, and that is why in order to decipher it it is necessary to take into account the context in which it appears. Myth is a sentence in a circular discourse, a discourse which is constantly changing its meaning: repetition and variation.[3]

This way of thinking brings us to dizzying conclusions. The social group which elaborates the myth *does not know* its meaning; he who tells a myth does not know what he is saying; he is repeating a fragment of a discourse, reciting a stanza of a poem whose beginning, end, and theme he does not know. The same thing happens with his listeners, and with the listeners to other myths. No one knows that this tale is a part of an immense poem: *myths communicate with each other by means of men and without men knowing it.* An idea which is not very far from that of the German Romantics and the Surrealists: it is not the poet who makes use of language, but rather language which speaks through the poet. There is a difference: the poet has the awareness of being an instrument of language, and I am not sure that the man telling the myth knows that he is the tool of a mythology. (Discussion of this point is premature: suffice it, for the moment, to say that for Lévi-Strauss the distinction is superfluous, since he thinks that awareness is an illusion.) The situation which *Le Cru et le cuit* describes is analogous to that of musicians performing a symphony while kept incommunicado and separated from each other in time and space: each one would play his fragment as if it were the complete work. No one among them would be able to hear the concert because in order to hear it one must be outside the circle, far from the orchestra. In the case of American mythology, that concert began millennia ago, and today some few scattered and moribund communities are running through the last chords. The readers of *Le Cru et le cuit* are the first to hear that symphony and the first to know that they are hearing it. But, are we really hearing it? We are listening to a translation or, more precisely, a transmutation: not the myth, but another myth. This is where the paradox of Lévi-Strauss's book and the paradox of myth lies. For the following reason: although the language of myth, as against the language of poetry, is easily translatable

40

into any language, real mythical discourse is, like music, untranslatable. In the myth, as I have already mentioned, articulate speech plays the same role as the phonemic system does in common discourse: myth makes use of words just as we, when we speak, make use of phonemes. Thus, the language of myth, the tale told in words, is an unconscious and presignifying structure upon which real mythical discourse is built. Therefore, Lévi-Strauss affirms that there is a real kinship between myth and music and not between myth and poetry. Myth as distinguished from poetry can be translated without any appreciable loss in the translation; similar to music, mythical discourse constitutes a language by itself, an untranslatable one. In my opinion, this analogy is imperfect: if there are two levels in myth, one properly linguistic and the other para-linguistic, in music we do not find the first level. On the other hand, on their first level, myth and poem are made up of words, and on the second, both are verbal objects, one made of mythemes and the other of metaphors or equivalences. I will return to this and will examine point by point the reasons which move Lévi-Strauss to uphold the peculiar identity between music and myth.

Le Cru et le cuit is barely the beginning of an enormous task: to determine the syntax of the mythology of the American continent. Lévi-Strauss rejects the method of historical reconstruction, not only for reasons of principle—although these are fundamental, as we have seen—but because it is impossible to determine the borrowings which Indo-American societies have made from one another from the end of the Pleistocene down to our day: America was a "Middle Ages without Rome." Its exploration rests instead on this evidence: the peoples who have worked out those myths "use the resources of a dialectic of opposites and mediations within a common concept of the world." Structural analysis thus confirms the assumptions of ethnography, archaeology, and history about the unity of American civilization. It is not difficult to infer that this research will lead to an even more ambitious undertaking: once the syntax of the American mythological system is determined, it will have to be placed in relation to that of other systems: the Indo-European, the Oceanic, the African, and the Mongol peoples of Asia. At this point, I will venture a hypothesis which is not at all gratuitous, since Lévi-Strauss's work gives us enough indications to postulate it: between the indo-European and American systems the relationship must be of diametrical opposition, such as is shown by the American *Ash boy* and the European Cinderella. This is not a unique example: the constellations of Orion and Corvus fulfill opposite though symmetrical functions among the Indians of Brazil and the Greeks. The same thing happens with the custom of charivari in Western Europe and the ritual commotion with which the same Brazilian Indians greet eclipses: in both cases we are dealing with a response to a disjunction or to an unnatural union, a sexual one in the Mediterranean and an astronomical one in South America.

The figure of the triangle is central to the thought of Lévi-Strauss. Therefore, although it may be presumptuous, it is not idle to wonder if the old opposition between East and West, the Indo-European and Mongol worlds, is not resolved in a mediation of America *prior* to the arrival of the Europeans on our continent. The American mythological system could be the point of contact, the mediation between two contradictory mythical systems. I am passing over an easy objection—"the American world is part of the Mongoloid region"—because the antiquity of man in America permits us to consider our Indian cultures as original creations, even though not autochthonous. The relationship between India and America would thus be one of symmetrical opposition, not only in space but in time as well: the Indian subcontinent is the point of real, *historical* convergence, between the

Mongoloid area and the Indo-European areas, while the American continent would be the point of *nonhistorical* coincidence between these two. Another contradictory relation: the Indo-European mythological system predominates in India, while American mythology has the same origin as the Mongoloid. The Indo-Aryan mediation places the accent on the Indo-European; the American places it on the Mongoloid. In the case of America, the perspectives of this assumption are wondrous, since Indo-Americans knew nothing of the mythical systems of the other two areas. We could say, in the manner of Lévi-Strauss, that civilizations communicate with each other without those who elaborate them being aware of it. The universality of reason—a greater reason than critical reason—will be demonstrated by the action of a thought which until recently we called irrational or prelogical.

I do not know if Lévi-Strauss would entirely approve of this interpretation of his thinking. I myself think it premature. In *Tristes Tropiques* and in other works he alludes to the problem of the relationships between Asia and America and leans toward an idea which is increasingly popular among researchers: the undoubtable analogies between certain traits of American, Chinese, and Southeast Asian civilizations cannot but be a consequence of migrations and cultural contacts between both continents. Lévi-Strauss goes further and proposes the existence of a subarctic triangle which would unite Scandinavia and Labrador with the north of America and the north of America with China and Southeast Asia. This circumstance, he says, would make the close "connection between the Grail cycle and the mythology of South American Indians" more understandable: the Celts and subarctic Scandinavian civilization would have been the transmitters. It is strange for him to appeal to history to explain these analogies: his entire effort is directed, rather, to seeing in this sort of coincidence not the consequence of history but an operation of the human spirit. Be that as it may, I don't believe I'm distorting him when I say that his work tries to resolve the heterogeneity of individual histories in an atemporal structure. To the pretensions of universal history, which vainly tries to reduce the plurality of civilizations to a single ideal direction—yesterday embodied in Providence, and today disembodied in the idea of progress—he opposes a vitalizing vision: there are no marginal peoples and the plurality of cultures is illusory, because it is a plurality of metaphors which say the same thing. There is a point at which all roads meet; this point is not Western civilization but the human spirit, which obeys, in all places and at all times, the same laws.

Le Cru et le cuit takes off from the examination of a Bororo Indian myth relating to the origin of storms, and shows its secret connection with other myths of the same Indians. Then he discovers the connections of this group of myths with those of neighboring societies and then explores an immense system which spreads over no less immense a territory. He reduces the relationships of each myth and each group of myths to "relational schemes" which in turn reveal affinities or isomorphisms with other schemes and groups of schemes. Thus arises a "multidimensional corpus" which is endlessly transformed and which makes its translation and its interpretation interminable. This difficulty is not too serious: Lévi-Strauss's purpose is not so much to study all American myths as it is to decipher their structure, isolate their elements and relational terms, discover the way in which mythical thought works. On the other hand, if myth is an object of perpetual metamorphosis, its interpretation obeys the same law also. Lévi-Strauss's book collects and repeats themes of his earlier books, not without changing them, and it advances themes and observations which his future books will work out—never exactly but rather in the manner of variations on a poem. His effort reminds me, on another level, of Mallarmé's: *Un Coup de dés* and *Le Cru et le cuit*

46

are both devices for meaning. This is not a fortuitous coincidence: Mallarmé anticipates many modern trends, in the realm of poetry, painting, and music as well as in that of thought. Mallarmé proceeds from poetic (primitive) thought toward logic, and Lévi-Strauss from logical thought to the primitive. At the same point in time that logical reason annexes the symbols of poetry, critical reason annexes the logic of the senses.

When he shows the relation between Bororo and Ge myths the French anthropologist discovers that they all have as their theme, which is never explicit, the opposition between the raw and the cooked, nature and culture. The myths of the jaguar and the wild pig, associated with those of the origin of the tobacco plant, refer to the discovery of fire and the cooking of foods. By means of the system of permutations which I have described above, Lévi-Strauss reviews in a summary way 187 myths in which this dialectic of opposition, mediation, and transformation is repeated. One after another, in a sort of dance—poetry and mathematics—the contradictory symbols follow one another: the continuous and discontinuous, the brevity of life and immortality, water and funeral ornaments, the fresh and the decayed, earth and sky, the open and the closed—the orifices of the human body turned into a symbolic system of ingestion and expulsion—the rock and the rotted log, cannibalism and vegetarianism, incest and parricide, hunting and agriculture, smoke and thunder. . . . The five senses are transformed into logical categories and upon this key to sensibility is superimposed an astronomy which is transformed into another key composed of the opposition of noise and silence, speech and song. All these myths are culinary metaphors, but in its turn, cooking is itself a myth, a metaphor of culture.

Three symbols caught my attention: the rainbow, the weasel, and fishing poison. The three are mediators between nature and culture, the continuous and the discontinuous, life and death, the raw and the decayed. The rainbow means the end of rain and the origin of illness; in both these ways it is a mediator: in the first instance because it is an emblem of the beneficent conjunction between sky and earth and in the second because it embodies the fatal transition between life and death. The rainbow is a homologue of the weasel, a lecherous and foul-smelling animal: one attribute ties it to life and the other to death (putrefaction). "Timbo" is a poison which the Indians use for fishing and thus is a natural substance used in an ambiguous cultural activity (fishing and hunting are transformations of war). In all three symbols the essential rupture or discontinuity between nature and culture, whose chief and central example is cooking, becomes thin and attenuated. Their equivocal character does not come solely from their being receptacles of contradictory properties, but rather from their being logical categories which are difficult to think about: in them the dialectic of oppositions is at the vanishing point. Because of their very transparency I would say they are unthinkable elements—something like the thought which thinks about itself. In order to recreate discontinuity, the rainbow is dissipated (the origin of chromatism, which is an attenuated form of natural continuity); poison belies its nature by its function (it is a deadly substance which gives life); and the weasel is transformed, in certain myths of heightened and sinister sexual coloration, from the homologue of illness and the "femme fatale" into a wetnurse and bearer of agriculture. It is not odd that at one point in his exposition, Lévi-Strauss associates the chromatism of the Wagnerian Tristan with poison and both of them with the unfortunate fate of Isolde the weasel.

The real theme of all these myths is the opposition between culture and nature as it is expressed in the human creation *par excellence*: the cooking of foods over a domestic fire. A Promethean theme with many

49

echoes: the schism between the gods and men, the eternal life of the cosmos and the brief life of human beings, but likewise the mediation between life and death, sky and water, plants and animals. It would be useless to try to list all the ramifications of this opposition since it encompasses every aspect of human life. It is a theme which leads us to the center of Lévi-Strauss's meditation: the place of man in nature. The position of cooking as an activity which at once separates and unites the natural world and the human world is no less central than the universal prohibition against incest. Both are prefigured by language which is what separates us from nature and what unites us to it and to our fellow men. Language signifies the distance between man and things as well as the will to erase it. Cooking and the incest taboo are homologues of language. The former is a mediation between the raw and the decayed, the animal world and the vegetable; the latter between endogamy and exogamy, wanton promiscuity and the onanism of a solitary individual. The model of both is the word, the bridge between the shout and silence, between the nonsignificance of nature and the insignificance of men. All three are screens which filter the anonymous natural world and turn it into names, signs, and qualities. They change the shapeless torrent of life into a discrete quantity and into families of symbols. In all three, the texture of the screen is made up of an intangible substance: death. Lévi-Strauss hardly mentions it. Perhaps his proud materialism keeps him from mentioning it. In addition, from a certain point of view, death is only another manifestation of immortal living matter. But how can we fail to see in that need to distinguish between nature and culture, in order to introduce a mediating term between the two of them, the echo and the obsession of knowing ourselves to be mortal?

Death is the real difference, the dividing line between man and the current of life. The ultimate meaning of all those metaphors is death. Cooking, the incest taboo, and language are operations of the spirit, but the spirit is an operation of death. Although the need to survive through nourishment and procreation is common to all living things, the wiles with which man confronts this inevitability make him a different being. To feel oneself and know oneself to be mortal is to be different: death condemns us to culture. Without it there would be no arts or trades: language, cooking, and kinship rules are mediations between the immortal life of nature and the brevity of human existence. Here Lévi-Strauss agrees with Freud and, at the other extreme, with Hegel and Marx. Closer to the latter two than to the former, in a second movement his thought tries to dissolve the dichotomy between culture and nature—not by means of work, history, or revolution, but by knowledge of the laws of the human spirit. The mediator between brief life and natural immortality is the spirit: an unconscious and collective device, as immortal and anonymous as a cell. Therefore, it seems to me a homologue of the rainbow, the fishing poison, and the weasel. Like these three active and funereal elements, it is by its origin on the side of nature, and by its function and its products on the side of culture. In it the opposition between death and life, the discrete significance of man and the infinite nonsignificance of the cosmos is almost erased. Facing death the spirit is life, and facing the latter, death. From the beginning, human understanding has been completely unable—because it is logically impossible—to explain nothingness by being or being by nothingness. Perhaps the spirit is the mediator. In the area of physics we reach similar conclusions; Professor John Wheeler, at a recent meeting of the Physical Society, asserted that it is impossible to locate an event in time or in space: before and after, here and there, are abstracts without meaning. There is a point at which "something is nothing and nothing is something." * . . . The spirit and the meaning of meaning are twin themes, but before dealing with them, I must examine the relations between myth, music, and a guest who was not invited to this banquet of Aesop which is the work of Lévi-Strauss: poetry.

* Tr. note: In English in the original.

III

*Dissonant intermezzo. Defense
of Cinderella and other digressions.
A verbal triangle: myth, epic, and poem.*

Le Cru et le cuit is an anthropology book which takes shape as a concerto. This is not the first time that a literary work has made use of musical terms and forms, though in general it has been the poets not the scientists who have taken their inspiration from music. It is true that ever since Apollinaire and Picasso the relationship between poetry and painting has been more intimate than that between poetry and music. I think that now our orientation is about to change, as well because of the evolution of contemporary music as of the renaissance of oral poetry. Both music and poetry will find a common ground in the new media of communication. In other respects several modern poets—Mallarmé, Eliot, and among ourselves, José Gorostiza—have given their creations a musical structure while others—Valéry, Pellicer, García Lorca—have emphasized the relationship between poetry and dance. For their part, musicians and dancers have always seen a model or archetype of their own creations in poetic forms. The kinship between poetry, music, and dance is a natural one: all three are temporal arts. Lévi-Strauss justifies the form of his book by the nature of the material he is studying and by the very nature of his interpretive method: he believes a real analogy exists not, as we might expect, between poetry and myth, but between myth and music. And furthermore, in the area of myth analysis we encounter "problems of construction for which music has already invented solutions." I am leaving aside this puzzling assertion and will limit myself to discussing the reasons which led Lévi-Strauss to posit a special relationship between mythical thought and musical thought.

The basis of his argument is crystallized in this sentence: "Music and myth are languages which, each in its own way, transcend the level of articulate speech." This assertion prompts two observations immediately. In the first place, music doesn't transcend articulate speech for the simple reason that its code or key—the musical scale—is not linguistic. In a strict sense, music is not language, although it might be proper to call it so as a metaphor, or by extension of the term. Music, like the other nonverbal arts, is a system of communication analogous to, not identical with, language. To transcend something one must go through that something and go beyond it: music does not transcend articulate speech because it does not go through it. The second observation: like myth, although in the opposite direction, poetry transcends language.* Thanks to the mobility of linguistic signs, words explain words: every sentence says something which can be said by another sentence; every meaning is a meaning which can be said in another way. The "poetic phrase"—a minimal rhythmical unit of the poem, the crystallization of the physical and semantic properties of language—is never a meaning: it is a final and irrevocable statement in which sense and sound merge. The poem is inexplicable except in terms of itself. On the one hand, it is an indissoluble totality and the tiniest change alters the whole composition; on the other, it is untranslatable: beyond the poem there is nothing but noise or silence, a senselessness or a meaning which words cannot name. The poem aims at a region at which, with the same insistence and the same impotence, musical signs aim. A dialectic between sound and silence, sense and non-sense, musical and poetic rhythms say something which only they can say, without ever saying it entirely. Therefore, like music, the

* In *El arco y la lira* [México: Fondo de Cultura Económica] (1956) [2nd rev. and enlarged ed., 1967], I have dealt with this topic at length, as well as with the relations between myth and poem. In this section and in others, I will be repeating what I say in that book, sometimes word for word.

poem "is intelligible and untranslatable language." I emphasize that it is not only untranslatable into other languages but also into the language in which it is written. The translation of a poem is always the creation of another poem; it is not a reproduction of, but a metaphor equivalent to, the original.

In sum, poetry transcends language because it transmutes that collection of mobile and interchangeable signs which is language into a final statement. Touched by poetry, language is more fully language, and at the same time, ceases to be language: it is a poem. An object made of words, the poem flows into an area which is inaccessible to words: sense dissolves, being and sense are the same. . . . Lévi-Strauss acknowledges in part what I have said: "In language the first non-significant character (the phonological one) is a medium and tool of the meaning of the second; the duality re-establishes itself in poetry, which regains the potential value of the meaning of the former in order to integrate it into the latter. . . ." He admits that poetry changes language, but he thinks that far from transcending it, it is thus more totally enmeshed within it: it descends from meaning to audible signs, it returns from the word to the phoneme. I will only say that it seems a perverse paradox to define Dante's, Baudelaire's, or Coleridge's activities in this way.

Music and myth "demand a temporal dimension to make their appearance." Their relation with time is peculiar because they assert it only to negate it. They are diachronic and synchronic: myth tells a story and, like a concerto, unfolds in the irreversible time of the performance; myth repeats itself, re-engenders itself, it is time which turns back on itself—what happened is happening now and will happen again—and music "immobilizes the time which is passing . . . so that when we listen to it we accede to a sort of immortality." In an earlier work, Lévi-Strauss had already emphasized the duality of myth, which corresponds to the distinction between language and speech, atemporal structure and the irreversible time of reciting. The analogy between music and myth is perfect only because it can be extended to the dance, and again, to poetry. The relations between dance and music are so close that no explanation is needed. In the case of poetry the synchronic and diachronic duality of language is reproduced, although on a higher plane since the second key or character, the signifying one, helps the poet to construct a third level which is not without similarities to that of music and, obviously, with the one Lévi-Strauss describes in *Le Cru et le cuit*. The time of the poem is chronometrical and likewise it is another time which is the negation of succession. In daily life we say: what's done is done; * but in the poem, what is done returns and takes shape again. The centaur Chiron tells Faust that the poet *is not chained to time: Achilles found Helen outside of time.* Outside of time? Rather in original time. . . . Even in epic poems and in historical novels, the time of the story eludes succession. Past and present in poems are not the past and present of history and journalism; they are not that which was nor that which happens but that which is being, that which is creating itself. Gest, gestation: a time which reincarnates and re-engenders itself. And it reincarnates in two ways: at the moment of the creation and at the moment of recreation, when the reader or the listener relives the images and rhythms of the poem and summons that shifting time which returns. . . . "Not all myths are poems, but in this sense, all poems are myths" (*El arco y la lira*, page 64). Poems and myths coincide in transmuting time into a special temporal category, a past which is always future and always ready to be present, to *present itself*. Thus, the relations of music with time are not essentially different from those of poetry and the dance. The reason is clear: these are three temporal

* Tr. note: In the Spanish: "Lo que pasó, pasó"; literally: "What's past is past."

arts which, in order to realize themselves, must negate temporality.

The visual arts repeat this dual relation, not with time but with space: a painting is space which refers us to another space. Pictorial space nullifies the real space of the painting; it is a construction which contains a space with properties analogous to those of the "frozen time" of music and poetry. A painting is space in which we see another space; a poem is a time which permits another time, at once fluid and motionless, to be seen. Architecture, more powerful than painting and sculpture, changes physical space even more radically: not only do we see a space which is not real but also we live and die in that second space. The stupa is a metaphor of Mount Merv but it is an incarnate, or more precisely, petrified, metaphor: we touch it and we see it as a real mountain. Theater, dance, cinema —temporal and spatial, visual and auditory arts—combine this pair of dualities: the stage and the screen are each a space which creates another space over which chronometrical time passes and which is reversible like the time of poetry, music, and myth.

Music and myth "operate on a double continuum, external and internal." In the case of myth, the external continuum consists in a "theoretically unlimited series of historical events, or events believed to be historical, from which each society takes a relevant number of happenings"; in regard to music, each musical system chooses a scale from the set of physically realizable sounds. It is almost unnecessary to mention that the same thing occurs in the dance: each system selects, from the movements of the human body and even from animals, a few which make up its vocabulary. The dance of Kerala (kathakali) uses a mimetic set while in European dance there is a sort of syntax of the leap and the contortion. In Sanskrit poetry the elephantine grace of the dancers is praised, and in the West, the swan and other birds are paragons of the dance. In poetry, the audible continuum of speech is reduced to some few meters, and it is well known that each language prefers only one or two: octosyllable and hendecasyllable in Spanish, alexandrine and nine-syllable line in French. That is not all: each versification system adopts a different method for making up its metrical canon: in Greco-Roman antiquity, quantitative versification, a syllabic one in the Romance languages, and an accentual one in the Germanic. Since the audible key is also semantic, each system is made up of a series of strict rules which operate on the semantic level as versification does on the level of sound. The art of versifying is an art of speech which does not combine all the elements of language, only a small group. In fact, myths and poems are alike to such an extent that not only do the former frequently use the metrical forms and rhetorical processes of poetry but the very material of myths—"the events" Lévi-Strauss alludes to—are also the material of poetry. Aristotle calls the plots or stories of the tragedies *myths*. When he wrote the *Fábula de Polifemo y Galatea*, Góngora not only gave us a poem which occupies in seventeenth-century poetry the place of *Un Coup de dés* in the twentieth century, but also offered us a new version of the myth of Cyclops.

The "internal continuum" is based on the listener's psychophysical time. The length of the tale, the recurrence of themes, surprises, parallelisms, associations, and divisions, provoke in the audience psychic and physiological reactions, mental and bodily responses: the myth's interest is "vital." Music affects our visceral system in an even more accentuated way: racing, jumping, motionlessness, convergence, divergence, the fall into the void, the ascent to the heights. I do not know if Lévi-Strauss has noticed that all these sensations can be reduced to this duality: movement and stasis. These two words evoke the dance, which is the real twin of music. The dance invites us to turn ourselves into music: it asks us to *accompany* it; and music invites us to dance: it asks us to *embody* it. The charm of music comes from the fact that the composer "holds back that which the listener expects, or gives him something he was not expecting." The word "surprise" expresses very imperfectly this feeling of "expectation frustrated or rewarded beyond what was foreseen." The same dialectic between the expected and the unexpected develops in poetry. It is a characteristic common to all the temporal arts and which even forms a part of oratory: an interplay between the before, the now, and the after. On the level of sound, the listeners are expecting a rhyme or a series of sounds and they are surprised that the poem resolves the sequence in an unforseen way. Nothing made this experience come alive for me more than to listen to a recital or poems in Urdu, a language which I do not know: the audience listened attentively and approved or was puzzled when the poet offered something which was different from what it expected. Etiemble says that poetry is a respiratory and muscular activity in which the lungs play as much of a part as the tongue, the teeth, and the lips. Claudel and Whitman insisted on the poem's rhythm of inhalation and exhalation. The listener and the reader reproduce all these sensations. Now, since in poetry "the sound must seem an echo of the sense," * those physiological

* Tr. note: In English in the original.

activities have a meaning; repetition and variation, separation and union, are processes which give rise to reactions at once psychical and physical. The dialectic of the surprise, Jakobson says, was defined by the poet Edgar Allan Poe, "the first to evaluate from the metrical and psychological points of view the pleasure which arises from the unexpected as it springs from what is expected, each unthinkable without its opposite."

In music and in myths there is "an inversion of the relationship between sender and receiver, since the latter discovers itself signified by the message of the former: music lives in me, I listen to myself through it. . . . Myth and the musical work are like an orchestra conductor whose audience are the silent performers." Again: poet and reader are two moments of the same operation; once the poem is written, the poet is alone and it is the others, the readers, who recreate themselves when they recreate the poem. The experience of creation is reproduced in opposite fashion: now the poem opens itself up before the reader. When he enters into these transparent halls he takes leave of himself and penetrates "another self" unknown until that moment. The poem opens for us the doors to strangeness and to recognition at the same time: I am that person, I was here, that sea knows me, I know you, in your thoughts I see my image multi-

plied a thousand times to the point of incandescence.
. . . The poem is a verbal mechanism which produces
meanings if and only if a reader or a listener sets it in
motion. The meaning of a poem is not in what the
poet meant to say but in what the reader says by
means of the poem. The reader is that "silent per-
former" Lévi-Strauss talks about. It is a phenomenon
common to all the arts: man communicates with himself, discovers himself and invents himself, by means
of the work of art.

If myths "have no authors and exist only when embodied in a tradition" the problem presented by music
is more serious: it has an author but we do not know
how music is written. "We know nothing about the
mental conditions of musical creation": why do only a
few put forth music while those who love music are
innumerable? This circumstance and the fact that "of
all languages only musical language is intelligible and
untranslatable" turn the composer "into a being similar to the gods, and music itself into the supreme mystery of human sciences—a mystery which keeps the secret of its own progress." Lévi-Strauss calls those who
like painting "fanatics"; this paragraph of his is an example of how fanaticism, but now a musical one,
aided by the fatal tendency toward eloquence of the
Romance languages, can lead even the finest spirits

astray. The mystery of musical creation is no more recondite or obscure than the mystery of pictorial, poetic, or mathematical creation. We still do not know why some men are Newtons and others Titians. Freud himself said that he knew little or nothing about the psychological processes of artistic creation. The numerical difference between those who create musical works and the fans of music is found in all the arts and the sciences: not everyone is a Whitman, a Darwin, or a Velázquez, but a great many understand and love their works. Nor is it correct to say that music is the only "intelligible and untranslatable" language. I've already said that the same is true of poetry and the dance. I will add now the examples of painting and sculpture: how can we translate African art, or the ancient art of Greece and Rome or of Japan? Each "translation" is a creation or transmutation called Cubism, Renaissance art, Impressionism. No work of art is translatable and all are intelligible—if we hold the key.

Lévi-Strauss does not make a distinction, which I think crucial, between *key* (a code or cipher) and *work*. The key to music is broader than the key to poetry, but it is narrower than the key to painting. The European musical system rests on a scale of notes, and it is more extensive than the French poetic system, which is based on the phonemic structure of that language; nevertheless, we need only cross the musical border and live in China or India for Western music to cease to be intelligible. The language of the visual arts is more extensive—not more universal—because its key, as Lévi-Strauss says, is "organized in the heart of sensible experience." The key to painting—colors, lines, volumes—is more sensory than intellectual and, therefore, it is accessible to a greater number of people independent of their language and their civilization. As the perfection and complexity of the key increases, its popularity decreases. The key to mathematics is narrower and more perfect than that of everyday speech. The linguistic key, precisely because of its perfection and complexity, is less extensive than the musical one, and so on through dance, painting, and sculpture. One may say that music uses a language of its own, "and that it is not susceptible to any general use," whereas the words of the poet are no different from those of the businessman, the cleric, or the revolutionary. Again: music is not articulate speech, a characteristic which joins it to painting and to the other nonverbal arts. In this sense, the language of colors and forms is also an exclusive domain of painting, although its key is less elaborate and perfect than that of music. Thus, the first distinction which ought to be made is that between verbal structures and nonverbal ones. Since language is the most perfect of communicative systems, verbal structures and not nonverbal ones are the model. In the linguistic universe proper, poetry and mathematics find themselves in a diametrically opposed situation: in the former, the meanings are many and the signs fixed; in the latter, the signs are variable and the meaning fixed. It is clear that music and other nonverbal arts share this characteristic of poetry. Ambiguity is the distinctive sign of poetry, and this poetic property turns music, painting, and sculpture into art.

If we go on from the keys to the works, Lévi-Strauss's opinion is even more unfair. The universality of a work does not depend upon its key but upon its message. I shall explain. I will grant for a moment that unfounded claim which sees in musical language a communicative system more perfect than the linguistic one: is Debussy more perfect and universal than Shakespeare, Goya, or the Bharhut reliefs which the French scientist so rightly admires? With a "sensory" key, El Greco creates spiritual work and Mondrian intellectual painting which borders on geometry and the binary theory of cybernetics. With a key which, according to Lévi-Strauss, owes little to natural sounds, Stravinsky composes the *Rite of Spring*, a poem about natural forces and rhythms. The universality and character of works of art does not depend upon the key but on that imponderable, real mystery which we call art or creation. The confusion between key and work perhaps explains Lévi-Strauss's disdainful opinions about abstract painting, serial and concrete music. As for the latter, one would have to say that, like electronic music, it is part of the search for an unconscious sound structure, or a structure of concrete natural units. This attempt recalls the "concrete logic of sensible qualities" in *La Pensée sauvage*. In another regard, in one of the most poetic and stimulating books I have read in recent years (*Silence*), John Cage says: "The form of the new music is different from the old, but it has a relationship with the great forms of the past, the fugue and the sonata, in the same way that these are related to each other." In art, every break is a transmutation.

A few pages later, led on by the devil of analogy, Lévi-Strauss observes in music the six functions which linguists assign to verbal messages. Again: those six functions also appear in the dance and, obviously, in the other arts. Although music and dance are not articulate speech, they are communicative systems which are very similar to language, and that is why their message is equivalent to one of the linguistic functions:

the poetic function. According to Jakobson, this function is not centered in the sender, the receiver, the contact between the two of them, the context of the message, or the key, but in the message itself. Thus, the poetic function distinguishes the Ajanta frescoes from the Sunday "comics": they are art, not because they tell us about Buddha's previous lives—a task performed better by the "jatakas"—but because they are painting. Other functions appear in that visual message—the emotive, the denotative, etc. —but the message is above all pictorial, and asks us to accept it as such. Now, the predominance of the poetic function in poetry does not imply that other functions may not appear in a poem; likewise, a verbal message can use the resources of poetic function without this meaning that it is a poem. Examples: advertisements, and at the other extreme, myths. Lévi-Strauss's book itself shows that myths are a part of the poetic function: myths are verbal objects and, therefore, use a linguistic key; this first key (which implies two levels: the phonemic and the meaning or semantic levels) helps mythical thought elaborate a second key; in its turn, *Le Cru it le cuit* offers a third key which permits the translation of the "concrete logic" of the myth into a system of symbols and logical propositions. This translation is a transmutation and has more than one similarity with poetic translation, as defined by Valéry: with different means it produces *similar* effects or outcomes. Perhaps one might object that my analogy forgets one difference: while poetic translation is made from one linguistic key to another, Lévi-Strauss's translation involves the passage from one system to another one, from the mythical tale to the symbols of mathematics and the propositions of science. I don't think so: in both cases the translation is transmutation, and in neither case do we leave the sphere of language—something which does not happen in music. Myths and equations are translated like poems: each translation is a transformation. The transformation is possible because myths, poems, and mathematical and logical symbols operate as systems of equivalences.

The poetic function (I am citing Jakobson again) transfers the principle of equivalence from the axis of selection to the axis of combination. The formulation of every verbal message comprises two operations: selection and combination. By means of the former, we choose the most adequate word from a group of words: "If *child* is the topic of the message: the speaker chooses between toddler, youngster, brat, etc."; then, he repeats the operation with the complement: is sleeping, dreaming, resting, is still; next, he combines his two choices: the child is sleeping. Selection is carried out "on the basis of similarity or dissimilarity, synonymy or antonymy, while combination, the construction of the sequence, rests on contiguity." Poetry turns this order around and "promotes equivalence to the rank of a constituent process of the sequence." Equivalence works on all levels of the poem: sound (rhyme, meter, accents, alliterations, etc.), and the semantic (metaphors and metonymies). Meta-language also uses "sequences of equivalent units and combines synonyms into sentence-equations. A equals A. But between poetry and meta-language there is a diametrical opposition: in meta-language, the sequence is used to build an equation; in poetry, the equation is used to build a sequence." * Lévi-Strauss's book is a meta-language and, simultaneously, a myth of myths; for the former he makes use of mythemes to build propositions which are, in a certain sense, equations; for the latter, he is taking part in the poetic function since he uses equations to work out sequences. In the case of the myths Lévi-Strauss examines, the order is inverted: secondarily they are a meta-language, and chiefly they are written within the

* Roman Jakobson, "Linguistics and Poetics," in *Style and Language*, ed. T. Sebeok [New York and London: Technology Press and John Wiley and Sons], 1960.

poetic function. Myths share in poetry and philosophy, without being either one or the other.

The notion of poetic function permits us to establish the intimate connection between myth and poem. If we observe the structure of one and the other we notice immediately a new similarity. Lévi-Strauss made a fundamental contribution when he discovered that the minimal units of a myth are larger than those of the discourse: phrases or sentences which crystallize bundles of relationships. In the poem we find an equivalent of the mytheme: what I have called, for lack of a better expression, "the poetic sentence." Unlike the unity of prose, the unity of this sentence, what constitutes it as such and turns it into an image, is not (solely) the meaning but (also) the rhythm. That is: the poem is made up of phrases or minimal units in which sound and sense are one and the same thing. These are sentences which are resolved into other sentences by virtue of the principle of equivalence which Jakobson alludes to and which turn the poem into a universe of echoes and analogies. Poems and myths open for us the doors to the forest of similarities.

Now I shall try to point out the difference between myth and poem. With regard to verbal signs, myth finds itself in a position equidistant from poetry and mathematics: as in the former, its meaning is plural; as in the latter, its signs are more easily interchangeable than in poetry. Within the poetic function, the lyric poem is found at one extreme and myth at the other. Between the lyric poem and myth there is an intermediate form: epic poetry. It is well known that epic poetry uses myth as its raw material or argument and that the decline of the epic genre (or rather: its metamorphosis into the novel) is due to the relative decline of myths in the West. I say "relative" because our myths have changed shape, and are called political, technological, and erotic utopias. Those myths are the substance of our novels and plays—from Don Juan, Faust, and Rastignac, to Swan, Kyo, Nadja, and Tim Finnegan. The borrowings between myth and epic are innumerable and almost all the resources of the former are used by the latter and vice versa. In sum, myth is situated on the frontier of the poetic function, a little beyond the novel, the epic poem, the short story, legends, and other mixed forms.

Myth is neither poem nor science nor philosophy, although it coincides with the first in its procedures (poetic function), with the second by its logic, and with the last by its aim of offering us an idea of the universe. Thus, just as the epic translates myth into fixed equivalences (meter and metaphors), philosophy translates it into concepts and science into sequences of propositions. Lévi-Strauss's book is, for this reason, a "myth of American myths," a poem, and, simultaneously, a book of science. . . . I confess that I cannot understand his impatience with poetry and poets. I once heard José Gaos say that the philosopher's arrogance is a contradictory passion, since it is a result of his total vision of the universe, and of the exclusivity of that vision. It is true: the philosopher's vision is an entirety from which many things are missing. Lévi-Strauss has cured himself of that arrogance with the antidote of the scientist's humility, but he still retains a certain philosophical ill-humor for that strange being which is poetry. For my part, I realize that I have devoted too many pages to this topic, and recognize, too late, that I have also committed the sin of fanaticism. Still, I shall add one more thing: as I write these lines I am hearing the first notes of a North Indian "raga": no, at no time did *Le Cru et le cuit* make me think of music. The pleasure which that book gave me evoked other experiences: reading *Ulysses* and the *Soledades*, *Un Coup de dés* and *A la Recherche du temps perdu*.

IV

Qualities and concepts: pairs and couples, elephants and tigers. The straight line and the circle. The pangs of progress. Ingestion, conversion, expulsion. The end of the Golden Age, and the beginning of writing.

Lévi-Strauss's work is a bridge suspended between two opposite landscapes: nature and culture. Within the latter, the opposition is repeated: *La Pensée sauvage* describes the thought of primitive societies and compares it with the thinking of historical ones. I should point out that the former is not the thought of primitive people but rather a mental behavior present in all societies and which in our own is manifested principally in artistic activity. Likewise, the adjective "historical" does not mean that primitive people lack a history; in the same way in which primitive thought occupies a marginal and almost underground place in our world, the idea of history does not have among the primitives the supreme place that we grant it. This repugnance toward historical thinking does not take away any rigor, realism, or coherence from primitive thinking. Once again: its logic is not different from ours in regard to mode of operation, although it may be different because of the goals to which it applies its reasoning. For example, among primitives the systems of classification which make up the general heading of taxonomy are no less precise than those of our natural sciences, and they are richer. Both the Australian herbalist and the European botanist introduce an order into nature, but while the former keeps in mind above all the sensory qualities of the plant—odor, color, shape, taste—and establishes a relationship of analogy between those qualities and those of other natural and human elements, the scientist measures and searches out relationships of a morphological and quantitative sort among the specimens, families, genera, and species. The former tends to work out total systems and the latter specialized ones. In both cases we are dealing with relations which are expressed by this formula: this is like that, or this is not like that. It has often been said that primitive thought is irrational, global, and qualitative, while scientific thought is exact, conceptual, and quantitative. This distinction, a constant theme of anthropological disquisitions at the beginning of the century, has proved illusory. Modern chemistry "reduces the variety of perfumes and smells to the combination, in differing proportions, of five elements: carbon, hydrogen, oxygen, sulphur, and nitrogen." Thus there appears a domain which was until now inaccessible to experimentation and research: that world of shifting characteristics which are only perceptible and definable by means of the concept of relationship. The scientist of the past measured, observed, and classified; primitive man feels, classifies, and combines; modern science penetrates the world of sensible qualities as does primitive science, thanks to the idea of combination, symmetry, and opposition. The taxonomies of primitives are not mystical or irrational. On the contrary, their method does not differ from that of "computers": * they are relational matrices.

Magic is a complete system and no less consistent within itself than science. The distinction between the two resides in "the nature of the phenomena to which each are applied." This difference is in turn the result of another: "the objective conditions in which magical and scientific knowledge appear." This explains why science gets better results than magic does. If this observation is correct (and I think it is), the difference between magic and science would be, in the first place, the precision, exactness, and perfection not of our senses or of our reason but of our equipment; and in the second place, the different goals of magic and science. As far as the former is concerned we shall presently see that the technical and operational inferiority of primitive thought is not so great, and that its

* Tr. note: In English in the original.

achievements have been no less important than those of science. The second observation confronts us with a problem of another sort: the contradictory orientation of societies. I will deal with this crucial topic below; here I will only say that magic poses problems which science ignores or which it prefers not to deal with for the present. In this sense it may seem impatient, and it is, but aren't the religions and philosophies of historical societies also impatient, and haven't they as few hopes of success as magic?

Magic and science proceed by analogous mental operations. In several brilliant and difficult chapters, Lévi-Strauss analyzes the totemic system—whose supposedly autonomous existence seems to him to be due to an error in his predecessors' point of view—in order to bring out the essential characteristics of this "concrete logic of sensory qualities." In a way not essentially different from ours, the primitive man establishes a relation between the sensible and the intelligible. The former refers us to the category of the signifier and the latter to that of the signified: qualities are signs integrated into significant systems by means of their relations of opposition and similarity. Far from being immersed in a dark world of irrational forces, the primitive lives in a universe of signs and messages. From this point of view he is closer to cybernetics than to medieval theology. Nonetheless, something separates us from that world: affectivity. The savage feels himself to be a part of nature and asserts his fraternity with the animal species. On the other hand, after believing ourselves to be the children of chimerical gods, we affirm the singularity and exclusivity of the human species for being the only one which has a history and which knows it. More sober and more wise, primitives distrust history because they see in it the beginning of the separation, the beginning of the exile of man adrift in the cosmos.

Primitive thought takes off from the minute observation of things and classifies all the qualities which seem pertinent to it; at once, it integrates these "concrete categories" into a system of relationships. The method of integration is, as we already know, binary opposition. The process can be reduced to these stages: observe, distinguish, and relate by pairs. These groups of pairs form a key which can then be applied to other groups of phenomena. The principle is no different from the one that rules the operations of the thinking machines of contemporary science. For example, the system of totemic classification is a key that can help make intelligible the system of food taboos of castes. As is well known, the diet of castes has always appeared as a radically different institution from totemism. Lévi-Strauss puts the transformational system into operation, and shows the formal connection between one diet and another, even though one is common in India and the other in Australia. This connection, once again, is not a historical one: so-called totemism and castes are operations of a mental structure which is collective and unconscious and which operates according to a combinatorial method of oppositions and similarities. Castes and totemism are expressions of a universal *modus operandi*, even though the former are a part of an historical society as extraordinarily complex as the Hindu, and the latter is primitive. The axis of this logic is the relation between the sensible and the intelligible, the particular and the universal, the concrete and the abstract. Primitives do not "participate" as Lévy-Bruhl thought; primitives classify and create relations. Their thinking is analogous, a characteristic which not only joins them with poets and artists in historical societies but also with the great hermetic tradition of Antiquity and the Middle Ages—that is: with the precursors of modern science. The analogy is a systematic one, and appears "under a double aspect: its coherence and its practically unlimited capacity for extension." In regard to the former, it withstands the criticism of the group; as for the second, the system can encompass all phenomena. It is a concrete logic because in it the sensible is significant; it is a symbolic logic because the sensible categories are in a relation of opposition or isomorphism with other categories and thus can build up a system of formal equivalences among the signs.

Primitive thought is opposed to history in two ways, as a science of the concrete and as an atemporal logic. The system of totemic classification is the best example of the resistance of primitive societies to the changes which all historical progression implies. Totemic classifications "comprise two groups: a natural, zoological and botanical, series, conceived in its supernatural aspect (the ancestors), and a cultural series, made up of human groups." The former is the origin of the latter but upon this temporal relation is superimposed another: since the first series coexists with the second one across time, there are continual relations between today and the beginning of the beginning. Totemic classification is a nontemporal rule which regulates social life and blocks the flight of the group toward history. A society which chooses the opposite road, that is, the one of succession and history, must renounce the double finite series of totemism and postulate a single and infinite series. For us, the idea of the flow of successive generations is a natural one; for an Australian this conception would be sui-

87

cidal: the group would disintegrate, classifications would dissolve. Lévi-Strauss does not say that primitive societies are outside of history; he points out that some societies choose the road of change whereas others persist in being faithful to an atemporal image, in which they see their origin and the invariable model of their occurring. The system of totemic classifications is not the only way to nullify or limit the corrosive action of history. All primitives try to "empty" the historical event "of its content": yesterday and tomorrow are the same, the end is identical with the beginning. Since in reality each instant is different and unique, myth offers a means of abolishing the singularity of history: today is not yesterday, but today, in order really to be and to prolong itself into tomorrow, must imitate yesterday. A yesterday outside of time and one which is the real today. The atemporal yesterday is the bridge between each instant. Ritual completes this function: it embodies myth, introduces the past effectively into the present, and in this way erases the historicity of the instant. In classification systems, in myths and rituals, history enters into the cycle of recurrent phenomena and thus loses its virulence. For us, the "image of the world" of this or that people is a consequence of its history; we ought to say, rather, that history is the projection of our image of the world.

Without denying its correctness it seems to me that this division between societies which have chosen to define themselves through history and societies which have preferred to do so through systems of classification, neglects an intermediate group. The idea of cyclical time is not exclusive with the primitives but also appears in many civilizations which we call historical. One could even say that only the modern West has identified itself fully and frantically with history, to the extent of defining man as a historical being, with obvious ignorance of and disdain for the ideas which other civilizations have created of themselves and of the human race. The vision of cyclical time encompasses the historical happening like a subordinate stanza in the circular poem which is the cosmos. It is a compromise between the atemporal system of primitives and the conception of a successive and unrepeatable history. China always combined the atemporal system, cyclical time, and historicity. The model was an archetypal past, the mythical time of the four emperors; historical reality was an anecdote from each period, with its wise men, its sovereigns, its wars, its poets, its saints, and its courtesans. Between both these poles, extreme immobility and extreme mobility, mediation was the circular movement of duality: yin and yang. An emblematic thinking, as Marcel Granet calls it, which emphasizes the reality of impersonal forces when it particularizes them and dissolves historical reality into a thousand colorful and fleeting anecdotes. In truth, China did not know history but annals. It is a civilization rich in historical tales, but their great historians never formulated what is called a philosophy of history. They did not need one, for they had a philosophy of nature. Chinese history is an illustration of cosmic laws and hence lacks exemplarity of its own. The model was atemporal: the beginning of the beginning. Meso-American civilization negated history more completely. From the Mexican high plateau to the tropical lands of Central America, for more than two thousand years, various cultures and empires succeeded one another and none of them had historical consciousness. Meso-America did not have history but myths and, above all, rites. The fall of Tula, the Toltec penetration into Yucatán, the disappearance of the great theocracies, and the wars and wanderings of the Aztecs were events transformed into rites and lived as rites. The Spaniards' conquest of Mexico will not be understood if it is not regarded as the Aztecs saw it and lived it: like a magnificent final rite.

India's attitude toward history is even more astonishing. I presume that it has been a response to the fact which has determined the life of men and institutions in the subcontinent for more than five thousand years: the need to coexist with other, different human groups in an unconquerable space which, though it seems immense, was and is fatally limited. India is a gigantic cauldron, and one who falls into it never comes out. Whether this has been the cause of the aversion to history or whether the reason is different, what is certain is that no other civilization has suffered the intrusions of history more, and none has negated it with such stubbornness. From the beginning, India set out to abolish history by means of the critique of time and to abolish the plurality of historical societies and communities by means of the caste system. The infinite mobility of real history turns into a shimmering and dizzying phantasmagoria in which men and gods whirl about until they merge in a sort of atemporal nebulosity; the varied world of events leads, or rather returns, to a neutral and empty region, in which being and nothingness are reabsorbed. Buddhism and Brahmanism negate history. For both, change, far from being a positive manifestation of energy, is the illusory realm of *impermanence*. Faced with the heterogeneity of ethnic groups—each with its own language, tradition, kinship system, and mode of worship—Indian civilization adopts an opposite solution: not the dissolution but the recognition of each particularity and its integration into a broader system. The critique of time and the caste system are the two complementary and antagonistic poles of the Indian system. By means of both, India aims at the abolition of history.

The model of the caste system is not historical, nor is it based only on the idea of the supremacy of one group over another, although this may have been one of its origins and the most important of its consequences. Its model is nature: the diversity of animal and vegetable species and their coexistence. When we saw a herd of wild elephants—the bull, cows, and their calves—in one of those "wild life sanctuaries" * which abound in this country, my guide told me: "Vegetarian animals like the elephant are polygamous, and the nonvegetarians"—he would not have said "carnivorous" for anything in the world—"like the tiger, are monogamous." This belief in the connection between food habits and the kinship system of animals throws more light on the caste system than reading a treatise. Lévi-Strauss is right: caste is not a homologue of totemism, but one could say that it is a mediation between the latter and history. It is a way

* Tr. note: In English in the original.

of integrating the flow of life into a nontemporal structure. . . . The minimal unit of the social system of India is not, as in modern societies, the individual but the group. This characteristic indicates again that their model is not historical society, but natural society, with its orders, species, families, and races. Individuals are prisoners of their caste: prisoners and beneficiaries. Fetal life, since a caste resembles nothing so much as a maternal womb. Perhaps this explains Hindu narcissism, the fondness of their art for curves, and of their literature for labyrinths, the femininity of their gods and the masculinity of their goddesses, their conception of the temple as a womb, and what Freud would call the infantile polymorphous perversity of the erotic games of their divinities and even of their music. I wonder if the psychological notion known as the "Oedipus complex" is entirely applicable to India; what in my opinion characterizes the Hindu is not the desire to return to the mother, but the impossibility of getting out of her. Was it always that way, or is this situation the result of external aggression which obliged Indian civilization to turn in on itself? Through disdain or through fear, abstracted or contracted, the Hindu has been insensible to the appeal of foreign countries: he does not seek the unknown abroad but in himself. In certain castes, the prohibition against traveling by sea was explicit and absolute. Nonetheless, in the past, the Hindus were great sailors, and the most beautiful monuments of the Pallava period—among the greatest gifts of Indian art to world sculpture—are found precisely in a port city, Mallapuram, which today is a fishing village.

The individual cannot get out of his caste, but the castes can change position, ascend or descend.* Social mobility is effected through a double channel. One, individual and within everyone's reach, is the renunciation of the world, the wandering life of the Buddhist monk and the Hindu sanayasi; the other, collective, is the slow and imperceptible movement of the castes, around and toward that empty center which is the heart of Hinduism: the contemplative life. To turn historical society into a natural society, and nature into a philosophical game, in a meditation on the one as against the unrealness of the plurality, is a splendid attempt—perhaps the most ambitious and coherent dream man has ever dreamt. But history, as if out of revenge, has begun to deal harshly with India. Over and over again she has been invaded by people who fought under the banner of movement and change: first, the Persians, the Greeks, the Scythians, the Ku-

* J. H. Hutton, *Caste in India*, London [Indian Branch, Oxford University Press, 4th ed.], 1963.

shans, and the White Huns; then, the Moslems with their one God and their brotherhood of believers; and finally, the Europeans with their progress which was no less universal and sectarian than the religion of the Prophet. The erosion of atemporal abstraction by change, the fall of the immobile being into the current of time, which was thought to be illusory. In the social sphere, the invasions did not modify the caste system but made it more rigid. To defend itself better, Indian civilization turned to contraction. Two universalities—different but equally exclusive: Islam and Protestant Christianity—surrounded and denaturalized a universal particularism. The Indian experiment, in other respects, had failed even without invasions: history in its crudest form, that is: demography, caused the system of coexistence to degenerate into one of the most unjust and useless systems of the modern era.

This failure makes me reflect on the fate of another experiment, diametrically opposite to the Indian but which is trying to resolve the same problem. I am referring to the United States. That country was founded by an exclusivist universalism: Puritanism and its politico-ideological outcome, Anglo-Saxon democracy. Once the territory was purged of alien elements—by the extermination and segregation of the indigenous population—the United States attempted to create a society in which the European national particularities, to the exclusion of others, would fuse in a "melting-pot." * The whole would be animated by history in its most direct and aggressive form: progress. That is, contrary to the Indian, the Anglo-American plan consists in a devaluation of European social and racial particularisms and in an overvaluation of change. But the non-European particularisms, especially the blacks, grew in such a way (outside the "melting-pot" and within society) that they now make any overdue attempt at fusion impossible. Thus, the "melting-pot" has ceased to be the historical model for the United States, and that country is condemned to segregation or to coexistence. For its part, the excessive valuation of progress has given rise to its being discredited by a large group, made up especially of young people and adolescents. This point is decisive. The revolt against abundance—in diametrical opposition to that of the underdeveloped countries, which is a revolt against poverty—is a rebellion against the idea of progress. The fondness of Anglo-American youth for drugs is not accidental. The country of action and strong drink suddenly discovers the attraction of contemplation and immobility. The drunkard is

* Tr. note: In English in the original.

not contemplative or passive, but talkative and aggressive; one who takes drugs is choosing immobility and introspection. The binge culminates in shouting, hallucination in silence. Drugs are a criticism of conversation, action, and change, the great values of the West and of its Anglo-American heirs. It is significant that the crisis in the foundations of American society should coincide with its greatest imperial expansion. It is a giant which is walking faster and faster along a thinner and thinner line.[4]

The plurality of societies and civilizations causes perplexity. Two contradictory attitudes can be taken toward it: relativism (this society is worth as much as that one) or exclusivism (there is only one worthwhile society—generally our own). The first attitude soon paralyzes us intellectually and morally: if relativism helps us understand others, it also prevents us from evaluating them, and forbids us to change them —them and our own society. The second attitude is no less false: how shall we judge others, and where is the universal and eternal criterion which can justify our decreeing that this society is good and that one bad? A descendent of Montaigne and Rousseau, of Sahagún and Las Casas, Lévi-Strauss's answer is a good one: respect other societies and change one's own.

This criticism culminates in the critique of the central idea which inspires our society: progress. Ethnography was born at almost the same time as the idea of history conceived as uninterrupted progress; it is not strange that it should be, simultaneously, the consequence of progress and the critique of progress. Naturally, Lévi-Strauss does not deny this: he situates progress in its historical context, the world of the modern West, and points out that it is not a universal historical law nor a standard of value applicable to all societies.

In general, progress is measured by dominance over nature, that is, by the amount of energy we have at our disposal. If science and technology were the decisive criteria, a civilization such as the Meso-American, which did not surpass the Neolithic as far as its tools were concerned, would not even deserve the name of civilization. Yet, the Meso-Americans not only left us a complex and refined art, poetry, and cosmology, but they also achieved remarkable feats in the realm of technology, above all in agriculture. In the area of science they discovered the concept of zero and worked out a more perfect, precise, and rational calendar than the Europeans. If we move from technology to morality, the comparison is even more in their favor: are we more sensitive, more honest, or more intelligent than the savage? Are our arts better than those of the Egyptians or the Chinese, and are our philosophers superior to Plato or to Nagarjuna? We live longer than a primitive but our wars take more victims than the medieval plagues. Even though infant mortality has diminished, the number of the needy increases every day—not in industrial countries but in those we euphemistically call underdeveloped, which make up two-thirds of humanity. It will be said that all this is a cliché. It is. The idea of progress has also become a cliché.

The best and the worst to be said about progress is that it has changed the world. The sentence can be turned around: the best and worst to be said about primitive societies is that they have hardly changed the world at all. Both variants need an amendment: we have not changed it as much as we think, nor the primitives as little. The people who raise the banner of progress have changed the social balance more than the natural one, although the latter is now beginning to be affected. The modifications have been internal and external. Internally, technical acceleration produced disturbances, revolutions, and wars; now it is threatening the psychic and biological integrity of the population. Externally, progressive society has destroyed innumerable societies and enslaved, humbled, and mutilated the survivors. Surely, the changes which it has introduced are enormous, very often beneficent, and, above all, undeniable. Its imbalances and its crimes are also undeniable. To say that does not imply any nostalgia for the past: every society is contradictory and there is none which escapes criticism. If progressive society is no better than other societies, neither does it have a monopoly of evil. The Aztecs, the Assyrians, and the great nomad empires of Central Asia were no less cruel, conceited, and brutal than we. Although we are outstanding in the museum of horrors, we are not number one.

Progress is our historical destiny; nothing is more natural than that our criticism be a criticism of progress. We are condemned to criticize progress in the same way that Plato and Aristophanes had to criticize Athenian democracy, Buddhism immobile being, and Lao-tse Confucian virtue and wisdom. The critique of progress is called ethnology. Ethnographic studies were born at the moment of the expansion of the West, and they immediately took a polemical form: defense of the indigenes' humanity stubbornly denied by their "discoverers" and exploiters, and a critique of the "civilizing" procedures of the Europeans. It is not by chance that the Spanish and the Portuguese, to whom belongs the dubious honor of having begun the conquest of the new world, have the right to a more secure honor: being the founders of ethnography. The descriptions the Portuguese made of the caste system in Travancore and other regions of South India, the Jesuits' descriptions of the civilizations of China and Japan, and the texts of the Spaniards about the institutions and customs of the American Indians are the first studies of modern times in ethnography and anthropology. In many cases, like Sahagún's, their method was as rigorous and objective as that of modern anthropologists who nowadays travel about the world equipped with tape recorders and other devices.

Lévi-Strauss says that ethnography is the expression of the "remorse" of the West. I don't know if he has noticed the Christian origin of this feeling. The critique of the excesses of progress is a critique of power and the powerful. Christianity was first in daring to criticize power and in exalting the humble. Nietzsche says that Christianity, precisely because it is a morality of remorse, put the finishing touches on our psychology and invented the examination of conscience, that operation which enables man to judge and condemn himself. Introspection is a Christian invention and always ends in a moral judgment, not of others but of oneself. The examination of conscience consists of putting oneself in the place of others, seeing oneself in the situation of the humiliated one or the vanquished:

the *other*. It is an attempt to recognize ourselves in the other, and in that way, to recover ourselves. Christianity discovered the other, and more than that, it discovered that ego only lives as a function of other. The Christian dialectic of the examination of conscience is repeated by ethnography not in the personal sphere, but in the social: to recognize a human being in the other, and to recognize ourselves not in the similarity but in the difference. In addition, without Christianity, the lineal idea of time (history) would never have been born. To that religion we owe progress, its excesses, and pangs of remorse: technology, imperialism, and ethnography.

There is a central aspect to the Hispano-Portuguese domination which I would like to point out. Iberian policy in the New World copies point by point the policy of the Moslems in Asia Minor, India, North Africa, and in Spain itself: conversion, whether voluntarily or by blood and fire. Though it may seem strange, the evangelization of America was a Moslem enterprise in its style and inspiration. The destructive fury of the Spaniards has the same theological origin as the Moslems'. When I saw the statues disfigured by Islam in the north of India, I immediately remembered the burning of codices in Mexico. The constructive passion of one and the other was no less than their destructive rage, and obeyed the same religious reason. The monuments left by the Moslems in India do not resemble those the Spanish and Portuguese erected in America, but their significance is analogous: first the temple-fortress (church or mosque) and then the great civil and religious creations. Architecture obeys a historical rhythm: occupation, conversion, and organization. Let us not forget, in addition, that the Moslem invasions on the Indian subcontinent and the conquest of America were undertakings which liberated part of the indigenous population which had been oppressed by the other: outcasts in India, and in America, people subjugated by the Inca and by the cruel Aztecs. Conquest and liberation are parts of the same process of conversion. I say conversion because the Moslems and their Portuguese and Spanish disciples did not intend to take in the other by respecting his otherness, like the anthropologist; they wanted to convert him, change him. Humanization consisted in transforming the infidel indigene into a brother in the faith. The subjects of Babur and those of his contemporary, Charles V, whatever their social situation, belonged to the same community if their faith was the faith of their masters. Mosque and church were, on Earth, the prefigurement of the world beyond: the point at which differences of race and rank were nullified, the place where otherness was erased. The Moslems and the Iberians confronted the problem of otherness by means of conversion, European Christians by means of extermination or exclusion. Examples: the annihilation of the aborigines in the United States and in Australia. In India, where it was physically impossible to eliminate the natives, there was no evangelization either, and the Christian population today does not reach ten million, while there are more than fifty million Moslems.* If we compare these practices with those of the Aztecs, we notice a difference: neither conversion in the Moslem and Hispano-Portuguese fashion, nor exclusion or extermination in the modern fashion, but divinization. Bloodthirsty and philosophical at the same time, the Aztecs resolved the problem of otherness by means of the sacrifice of prisoners of war. Physical destruction was likewise a transfiguration: the victim achieved the immortality of

* The slaughter of Indians in Argentina, Uruguay, and Chile was a result of a deliberate and irrational imitation of Anglo-American practices: progress was identified with the extermination of the indigenous population and with European immigration. The chief theorist of this policy was Domingo Faustino Sarmiento, one of the official worthies of Latin America. The motto "to govern is to populate" depopulated those three countries.

104

the sun. Conversion, exclusion, extermination, ingestion . . .

For a Chinese or an Australian aboriginal the critical function did not present the theoretical difficulty it does to us: judgment sprang from the comparison between the present and the atemporal model, whether this was the mythical past of the Yellow Emperor or the series of divine animal ancestors. The same can be said of all other civilizations: the Golden Age was a point of reference and it did not matter whether it was located before, after, or outside of history. It was an unchanging model. In a society which ceaselessly transforms itself, the Golden Age, the ideal reference system, also changes. For this reason, our critique is also utopian thinking, the search for a Golden Age which ceaselessly transforms itself. Our ideal society changes continually and has no fixed place in time or in space; daughter of criticism, it creates itself, destroys itself, and recreates itself as does progress. A permanent beginning-again: not a model but a process. Perhaps for this reason modern utopias tend to be presented as a return to that which does not change: nature. The seductiveness of Marxism consists in its being a philosophy of change which promises us a future Golden Age the germ of which was already present in the most distant past, "primitive communism." It thus combines the prestige of modernity with that of archaism. Condemned to change, our utopias shift between paradises which preceded history and the metropolises of technology's steel and glass, between the prenatal life of the fetus and an Eden of robots. And either way our paradises are hellish: some resolve themselves in the tedium of incestuous nature, others in the nightmares of the machine.

Perhaps the real Golden Age is not in nature or in history but in between them: in that instant when men establish their group with a pact which simultaneously unites them among themselves and unites the group with the natural world. Rousseau's thought is seminal and Lévi-Strauss points out that many of contemporary anthropology's discoveries confirm his intuitions. But the image the Genevan philosopher constructed of the earliest age does not match prehistorical reality: Paleolithic hunters have left an extraordinary art, but that society is not exactly an ideal model. On the other hand, Lévi-Strauss thinks that the neolithic period—precisely before the invention of writing, metallurgy, and the birth of urban civilization with its debased masses and its monarchs and its bloodthirsty priests—is what comes closest to our idea of a Golden Age. The men of the neolithic era—

according to Gordon Childe, most probably the women —invented the arts and crafts which are the foundation of all civilized life: ceramics, weaving, agriculture, and the domestication of animals. These discoveries are crucial and perhaps are superior to those achieved in the last six thousand years of history. Thus, what I noted above is confirmed: primitive thought is not inferior to ours either in terms of the precision of its methods or in terms of the importance of its discoveries. Another point in favor of Neolithic man: none of his inventions are injurious. We cannot say the same about historical societies. Without thinking of the uninterrupted progress in the art of killing, have we reflected on the ambivalent function of writing? Its invention coincides with the appearance of the great empires and the construction of monumental projects. In an impressive passage, Lévi-Strauss shows that writing was the property of a minority and was not used so much for communicating knowledge as for dominating and enslaving men. It was not writing but the printing press which liberated men. It liberated them from their superstition of the written word. I shall add that, in reality, the printing press wasn't the liberator, but the bourgeoisie, which made use of this invention to break the monopoly of sacred knowledge and spread *critical* thinking. Marshall McLuhan's notion that the printing press transformed the West is puerile: techniques do not change society but the coming together of men and tools does.

In another essay I have dealt with written expression in relation to verbal expression: writing denatures the dialogue between men.* Although a reader may agree or disagree, he is unable to question the author and to be heard by him. Poetry, philosophy, and politics—the three activities in which speech develops all its powers—suffer a sort of mutilation. If it is true that thanks to writing we have at our disposal a universal, objective memory, it is also true that it has increased the passivity of our citizens. Writing was the sacred knowledge of all bureaucracies, and even today it is unilateral communication: it stimulates our receptive capacity and at the same time neutralizes our reactions, paralyzes our criticism. It interposes a distance between us and the one who is writing—be he philosopher or despot. But then I don't think that the new media of oral communication in which McLuhan and others place so much hope shall succeed in reintroducing real dialogue among men. Despite their restoring to the word its verbal dynamism—something which contemporary poetry and literature have still not taken advantage of fully—radio and television increase the

* *Los signos en rotación*, Buenos Aires [Sur], 1965.

distance between the one speaking and the one who is listening: they turn the former into an all-powerful presence, and the latter into a shadow. They are, like writing, tools of domination. If there is a grain of truth in the view of the Neolithic age as a happy one, that truth consists not in the justice of its institutions, about which we know exceedingly little, but rather in the peaceful nature of its discoveries, and above all, in the fact that those communities knew no other form of relationship than the personal one of man to man. The true foundation of all authentic democracy and socialism is, or ought to be, conversation: men face to face with each other. On this topic, we are indebted to Lévi-Strauss for some unforgettable passages, such as those where he discovers how well founded Rousseau's guess was: that the source of authority, in the simplest society, is not coercion by the powerful, but mutual consent. Driven on by his enthusiasm, Lévi-Strauss even says that the "Golden Age is in ourselves." A marvelous but ambiguous statement. Is he referring to an internal and personal state or to the possibility of returning with new technological means to a sort of Golden Age of the industrial era? I fear that, in the second sense, this is a utopian idea: we have never been farther from person-to-person communication. Alienation, if this overworked word still retains any sense, is not solely a result of social systems, be these capitalist or socialist, but rather of the very nature of technology: the new media of communication. They deform the speakers; they magnify authority, make it inaccessible—a god that speaks but does not listen— and thus they rob us of the right and the pleasure of a reply. They suppress dialogue.

V

Practices and symbols. Yes or no, and the more or less. Man's unconscious and the machines'. Signs which destroy each other: transfigurations. Taxila.

Lévi-Strauss has always declared himself a disciple of Marx (disciple, not echo). A materialist and determinist, he thinks the institutions and ideas a society has about itself are the products of an underlying unconscious structure. Nor is he insensitive to the historical program of Marx and, if I'm not mistaken, he believes socialism is (or could be) the next stage in the history of the West and perhaps of the whole world. If he conceives of society as a system of communications, it is natural that private property would seem to him an obstacle to communication: "In language," Jakobson says, "there is no private property: everything is socialized." . . . Having said this I don't see how we can call him a Marxist without stretching the meaning of the term. For example, I am not sure he shares the theory which sees culture as a simple reflection of material relationships. It is true he says he accepts with no difficulty the primacy of the economic structure over others, and in *La Pensée sauvage* he asserts that these latter are really superstructures; he even goes on to say that his studies could be called a "general theory of superstructures." But then he limits economic determinism's validity to historical societies; as for the nonhistorical ones, he assures us that blood ties play the decisive role in them as the means of economic production do in historical societies. He bases his assertion on some of Engels' opinions in a letter to Marx. I'm not trying to intervene in a difficult and, in any case, marginal question, but I confess that his idea of the relations between "praxis" and thought strikes me as quite different from the Marxist conception.

In *La Pensée sauvage* he distinguishes between "practices" and praxis; the study of the former, which are characteristic of types of life and forms of civilization, is the domain of ethnology, and the study of the latter is history's. Practices would be superstructures. Between praxis and "practices" there is a mediator: "the conceptual framework by means of which a material and a form are achieved as structures at once empirical and intelligible." To my way of thinking this idea eliminates the notion of praxis, or at least, gives it a different meaning from the one it has in Marxism. The immediate and active relation of man with things and with other men is indistinguishable, according to Marx, from thinking: "The controversies about the reality or the non-reality of thought as separate from *practice* belong to the realm of scholasticism" (*Theses on Feuerbach*). Praxis and thought are not different entities and both are inseparable from the objective laws of social reality: the means of production. Marx is opposed to the old materialism, writes Kostas Papaioanno, because it ignores history. For Marx, nature is historical, so that his materialism is a *historical concept of matter*. The old materialism "affirmed the priority of external nature, but an objective nature, independent of the subject, does not exist." The sensory world is not a world of objects: it is the world of praxis, that is, of matter modeled and changed by human activity. The function of praxis is "to modify nature historically."

If Marxism is a historical conception of nature, it is also a materialist conception of history: praxis, "the real vital process," is man's being, and his consciousness is nothing but the reflection of that matter which praxis has turned into history. Human consciousness and thought are products not of nature but of historical nature, that is of society and its means of production. Neither nature nor thought by itself defines man; he is defined rather by practical activity, work: history. Lévi-Strauss says, at the end of *La Pensée sauvage*, that praxis can only be conceived of provided that it exists *before* thought, under the "guise of an objective structure of the psyche and of the brain." The spirit is something given and constituted from the beginning. It is a reality insensitive to history and to the means of production because it is a physicochemical object, an apparatus which combines the signals and responses of the brain cells to external stimuli. In praxis, the spirit repeats the same operation as at the moment it works out the practices: it separates, combines, and sends. Spirit transforms the sensible into signs. In Marx's conception, I detect the primacy of the historical: the means of social production; in Lévi-Strauss's, the primacy of the chemico-biological: a means of natural operation. For Marx, consciousness changes with history; for Lévi-Strauss, the human spirit does not change: its realm is not that of history but of nature.

From this perspective we can better understand his argument with Sartre and the mistake which joins and divides them. For Sartre the opposition between analytical reason and dialectical reason is real because it is historical; I mean: each of them corresponds to a different history and means of production, or more precisely, to different stages of the same history. Dialectical reason negates analytical reason and thus encompasses and transcends it. It is not reason in movement as Lévi-Strauss would have it, but the movement of reason. That movement changes it and effectively turns it into another reason: what analytical reason says is understood by dialectical reason while the latter speaks in a language incomprehensible to the former. Dialectical reason places analytical reason in its historical context and, when it relativizes it, integrates it into its own movement. On the other hand, analytical reason is incompetent to judge dialectical reason. . . . The defect in Sartre's position is that of every dialectic as soon as it stops resting on a foundation. Dialectical reason certainly can understand and judge analytical reason, and the latter is incapable of understanding and judging it; but, does dialectical reason understand itself and can it justify itself? Dialectical reason is an illustration of the paradox of movement: the Earth moves about a sun which seems motionless and which, for the purposes of earthly movement, actually is. Now then, dialectic, ever since Hegel, has lacked a sun: if dialectic is the movement of the spirit, there is a reference point according to which movement is movement. The foundation of the dialectic is nondialectical, for if it were otherwise, there would be no movement, no dialectic. Marx never clearly explained the relationship between his method and Hegel's dialectic, although he promised he would do so in a few pages. Thus, we lack the point of reference between dialectic and matter. Engels tried to remedy this omission with his disquisitions on the dialectic of nature which are today unacceptable to science, as Sartre himself, among others, has shown.*

Materialist dialectic lacks a foundation and has no reference system which would permit it to be understood and, literally, measured. Contemporary science admits that the observer changes the phenomenon but it knows that he changes it and it can calculate that change. If this were not so, there would be no observation or determination of the phenomenon. In fact, the very notion of objective phenomena would disappear. It could be objected that the point of reference of Marxism is the dialectical leap: thanks to negation we can understand affirmation. It would be a "progressive-regressive" operation, to use Sartre's vocabulary: dialectical reason understands analytical reason and thus rescues it. I would observe that negation illuminates affirmation only the better to erase it. If dialectic claims to find its foundation not before but after the

* See Maximilien Rubel's note to Marx's epilogue to the second German edition of *Capital* (*Oeuvres de Karl Marx*, vol. I, *La Pléiade* edition). Likewise, the essay of Kostas Papaioannou: "Le mythe de la dialectique" (*Contrat Sociale*, September–October, 1963).

leap, it encounters this difficulty: that "after" immediately turns into a "before." Dialectic seemed to us like a movement, and now it becomes a motionless frenzy. In sum, Sartre's criticism is a two-edged sword: it settles the contradiction between matter and dialectic in the latter's favor. Marxism ceases to be materialism, and dialectic becomes a tortured soul in search of its body, in search of its foundation.

Lévi-Strauss points out that Sartre turns history into a refuge for transcendence and that, therefore, he is guilty of the crime of idealism. Perhaps he is correct with this reservation: it would be a transcendence which destroys itself because each time it transcends itself it nullifies itself. Yet, Sartre is right when he says that dialectic transcends analytical reason. What happens is that, when it transcends it, it invalidates itself as reason. To restore its rational dignity, dialectic must carry out an operation inconsistent with its nature: to appear before the judgment of analytical reason. Something which is impossible because, as we have seen, analytical reason does not understand the language of the dialectic: it lacks a historical dimension just as the dialectic lacks a foundation. In other respects, the question about the foundation or sufficient cause also bears upon Lévi-Strauss's reason: what is the reason for the physicochemical processes of the brain? This inquiry repeats on another level the question at the beginning: what is the meaning of meaning? At one and the other extreme of Lévi-Strauss's system, the ghost of philosophy appears. Since I intend to return to this matter, I will only say now that the quibble between Lévi-Strauss and Sartre consists in the fact that both have changed the Marxist notion of praxis: the former in favor of a nature outside of history and the latter in favor of a purely historical dialectic. For Lévi-Strauss, history is a category of reason; for Sartre, reason is a historical category. Sartre is a pure historicist and his conception recalls the ratio-vitalism of Ortega y Gasset, with the difference that it is not generations but classes which are the embodiments of historical movement. Lévi-Strauss is a materialist, also a pure one, and his thinking continues eighteenth-century materialism, with the difference that for him matter is not substance but a relation. This hallmark turns him into a thinker not of the first half of this century, like Sartre, but of the second: the one beginning now.

More to the point than Marxist criticism is that of the English anthropologist Edmund Leach.* Here we descend from scholasticism to the firm ground of common sense. Leach begins by pointing out that the im-

* "Telstar et les aborigènes: ou 'La Pensée sauvage,' " [Annales (Paris), no. 6] (1964).

portance of Lévi-Strauss's work lies in that it proposes to explain the "non-verbal content of culture as a system of communications; therefore, it applies to human society the principles of a general theory of communication." That is: the binary structure of phonology and electronic brains which make up messages by combining negative and positive impulses. The binary distinction is a "first class analytical tool but it has certain disadvantages. One of them is that it tends arbitrarily to undervalue problems related to values." The latter can be approached with greater probability of success by *analog computers*.* While these mechanisms respond to questions in terms of more or less, machines which use the binary system reply only with a *yes* or *no*. Leach illustrates his observation with the totemic classification system as it has been defined by Lévi-Strauss. According to the French anthropologist, aborigines do not choose this or that animal species for their totem because of its usefulness but rather because of its qualities and peculiarities, that is, because the qualities can more easily be defined—because of their ability to form conceptual pairs. The British functionalists assert that species become totemic on account of their utility; for example: because they are

* Tr. note: In English in the original: "analogical computers."

edible. Lévi-Strauss holds that they are categories of classification: they become totemic because they are thinkable, not because they're edible. Though his solution is more universal and simpler than the other one —above all if we accept the idea that totemism is not an isolated institution but an aspect of a general system of coordination of the universe and of society—it presents one inconvenience. The British theory is crude and ingenuous: the animal is sacred because of its beneficial or noxious function; Lévi-Strauss's theory shows us the formal reason of totemic classifications but does not touch on something which is essential: *why* are totemic species sacred? The same observation can be applied to food or sexual taboos. It is not sufficient to say that Europeans do not eat the meat of dogs or Moslems the meat of pigs; the first taboo is implicit and the second is explicit. This difference, according to Leach, cannot be explained by the binary method. In sum, Lévi-Strauss "shows us the logic of religious categories and at the same time disregards precisely those aspects of the phenomenon which are specifically religious." I think Leach is right, but would point out that, without meaning to, his penetrating criticism evokes a participant whom he and Lévi-Strauss have expelled from the anthropological symposium: phenomenology of religion.

Leach does not deal with the foundations of Lévi-Strauss's method: in certain cases he merely proposes to substitute for binary analogy another more refined one. For my part, I would ask if the basic principle is valid: is the general theory of communication a universal model? At first sight, the reply must be in the affirmative, at least in the sphere of living things, as contemporary genetics has shown. But still, it is right to assume that as has always happened in the history of science, sooner or later a difference will appear which will make the model inoperative. I have another doubt: machines think, but they do not know that they are thinking; the day they come to know that, will they still be machines? I will be told that all men, merely because they talk, are thinking, and yet, only a very few, and on very rare occasions, are aware that each time they pronounce a word they are carrying out a mental operation. I would reply that it is enough for one single man to be aware that he is thinking for everything to change: what distinguishes thought from all other operations is its capacity to know that it is thought. As soon as I wrote this sentence, I noticed in it a certain inconsistency; my idea presupposes something which I have not proved, and which is not easy to prove: an ego, a consciousness. If thought is what is aware that it is thinking—and it cannot be anything else—we are confronting a general property of thought; therefore, if machines think, one day they will know that they think. Consciousness is illusory and consists of a simple operation.[5] I would counter and dare to offer another comment: machine logic is inflexible, infallible, and indisputable, while ours is subject to enfeeblement, aberrations, and hallucinations. As Zamiatin said: man is sick and his sickness is called fantasy: "Each stroke of a piston is an immaculate syllogism, but who has ever heard a pulley tossing and turning in bed for nights on end or brooding when it is idle?" I would attribute this difference to the fact that we have different unconsciouses: either machines lack something or we have something extra. Or is this also an illusion?

Lévi-Strauss introduces a singular distinction between the unconscious and the subconscious. The latter is the depository of images and memories, "an aspect of memory"—something like an immense, disorderly, and jampacked archive. The unconscious, on the other hand, "is always empty"; it receives the "pulsations," emotions, representations, and other external stimuli and organizes and transforms them "as the stomach does with the foods which pass through it." Despite the fact that Freud thought that progress in chemistry would make lengthy psychoanalytical treatment unnecessary, his conception of the unconscious is completely opposed to Lévi-Strauss's: for Freud, the psychic processes, both the unconscious and subconscious ones, have a *goal.* This goal gets various names: desire, the pleasure principle, Eros, Thanatos, etc. Many have emphasized the relationship of this psychological unconscious with the economic structures of Marx, which are also unconscious, and likewise possessed of a direction. The unconscious and history are moving forces which proceed independently of the will of men. Far from being empty apparatuses which change what they receive from the outside into signs, they are full realities which endlessly change man and transform themselves. The living material of Freud aspires to the nirvana of inert matter; it wants to come to rest at unity but it is doomed to move and divide, to desire and hate the forms it engenders. The historical man of Hegel and Marx wants to suppress his otherness, to be one again with others and with nature, but he is doomed to change himself constantly and to change the world. In a brilliant book (*Love Against Death*), Norman O. Brown has shown that the energy of history can also be called repressed and sublimated Eros. Historical dialectic, whether Hegel's or Marx's, reappears in Freud's theory: affirmation and negation are concepts

125

which match those of libido and repression, pleasure and death, activity and nirvana.

The materialisms of Freud and Marx do not do away with the idea of goal; they situate it on a deeper level than that of consciousness and thus they strengthen it. Alien to consciousness that goal is actually an indisputable force. At the same time, Marx and Freud offer a solution: as soon as man becomes aware of the forces which move him, he is in a position, even if not to be free, at least to establish a certain harmony between what he really is and what he thinks he is. This consciousness is an active knowing: for Marx, Promethean and heroic, it is social action— praxis conscious of itself—which transforms the world and man; for Freud, the pessimist, it is the continually upset balance between desire, and repression. Thus, the difference between these two conceptions of the unconscious and Lévi-Strauss's rests on the fact that in the first case, man comes to the knowledge of an active unconscious, one possessed of a goal, while in the second case, he contemplates an apparatus which knows no activity other than repetition, and which lacks a goal. It is a *knowledge of the void.*

In his commentary on *Les Structures élémentaires de la parenté,* cited at the beginning of these pages,

Georges Bataille decried the fact that Lévi-Strauss hardly deals with the theme of the relationship between the exchange of women and eroticism. The taboo-gift duality also appears here: it is a sort of wavering between horror and attraction which is always resolved in violence, whether internal (renunciation) or external (aggression). The play of passions constitutes the specific side of the phenomenon, though other circumstances—economic, religious, political, magical ones—come together in determining it. In other words, Bataille asked that the incest taboo and its counterpart, kinship and matrimonial rules, be explained not only as a form of giving, a particular expression of the theory of the circulation of goods and signs, but that it be explained by that which distinguishes it from other systems of communication. I will add: eroticism is communication, but its specific elements, aside from the fact that they isolate it and set it in opposition to other forms of exchange, invalidate the very idea of communication. For example, to say that marriage is a relation between signs which designate names (ranks and lineages) and values (display, children, etc.) is to omit that which characterizes it: being a mediation between renunciation and promiscuity, and thus creating a closed and legal environment in which erotic play may develop. Now then, if women are signs bearing names and goods, we ought to add that they are passional signs. The very dialectic of pleasure—gift and possession, desire and vital expenditure—endows these signs with a contradictory meaning: they are the family, order, continuity, and they are at the same time the unique, the disordered, the erotic moment which breaks continuity. Erotic signs destroy meaning—they burn it and transfigure it: meaning returns to being. And in the same fashion, when the carnal embrace carries out communication it invalidates it. As in poetry and music, the signs no longer signify: they are. Eroticism transcends communication.

Bataille points out that the incest taboo is also linked to two other negations by which man opposes his original animality: work and the awareness of death. Both confront us with a world which Lévi-Strauss prefers to ignore: history. Man makes, and in making unmakes, himself, dies—and he knows it. I wonder: is man an operation or a passion, a sign or a history? This question can be repeated, as we have seen with Lévi-Strauss's other studies on myths and primitive thought. With extraordinary insight he has discovered the logic which rules them, and has shown that, far from being confused psychic aberrations, or manifestations of illusory archetypes, they are systems which are coherent and no less rigorous than those of science. On the other hand, he omits the description of their concrete and specific content. Nor is he interested in the particular meaning of those myths and symbols within the human group which elaborates them. When turned into a simple combination, the phenomenon evaporates and history is reduced to gibberish, and to a ghostly feat. Someone will tell me a scientist has no reason to wander in the labyrinths of phenomenology or of the philosophy of history. I think just the opposite. Lévi-Strauss's work fascinates us because it breaks into the double and endless monologue of phenomenology and history. That interruption is, at the same time, historical and philosophical: the negation of history is a response to history and philosophy reappears as a critique of meaning—as a critique of reason.

Ricoeur has found a surprising resemblance between Kant's system and Lévi-Strauss's: like the former, the latter postulates a universal understanding ruled by laws and unvarying categories.* The difference would

---

* I note, in passing, that Martin Heidegger, in *Being and Time*, attempted something similar, only not in the sphere of understanding, but in that of temporality. Therefore, people have with justification objected to confusing his thinking

be that the French anthropologist's is an understanding without a transcendent subject. Lévi-Strauss accepts the validity of the comparison and, without negating it, points out its limitations: the ethnologist does not start from the hypothesis of universal reason, but from the observation of specific societies, and little by little, through classification and observation of each distinctive element, draws the lines "of a general anatomical structure." The result is an image of the form of reason and a description of its function. The similarity pointed out by Ricoeur ought not make us forget one difference which is no less decisive: Kant attempted to discover the limits of understanding; Lévi-Strauss dissolves understanding into nature. For Kant there is a subject and an object; Lévi-Strauss erases this distinction. In place of the subject he posits an "us" made up of particularities which oppose each other and combine with each other. The subject saw himself and the judgments of universal understanding were his. The "us" cannot see itself: it has no "self"; its intimacy is exteriority. Its judgments are not its

---

with existentialism's. Lévi-Strauss's formalism prevents me from comparing his conceptions with Heidegger's; but that is not so for the old nominalism: in its system the universe is resolved into signs, names. It would be worth while to explore these affinities further.

own: it is the vehicle for judgments. It is strangeness in person. It cannot even know itself to be a thing among things: it is a transparency through which a thing, the spirit, looks at other things and lets them look at it. When he abolishes the subject, Lévi-Strauss destroys the dialogue of consciousness with itself, and the dialogue of the subject with the object.

The history of Western thought has been the history of the relations between being and meaning, the subject and the object, man and nature. After Descartes, the dialogue was altered by a sort of exaggeration of the subject. This exaggeration culminated in Husserl's phenomenology and Wittgenstein's logic. The dialogue of philosophy with the world became the interminable monologue of the subject. The world was silent. The growth of the subject at the expense of the world is not limited to the idealist current: Marx's historical nature, and the "domesticated" nature of experimental science and of technology also display the stamp of subjectivity. Lévi-Strauss breaks brutally with this situation and inverts the terms: now it is nature which speaks with itself, through man and without his being aware. It is not man but the world which cannot come out of itself. If it did not force the language too much, I would say that the universal understanding of Lévi-Strauss is a transcendent object.

"Man in himself" is not even inaccessible: he is an illusion, the fleeting key of an operation. A sign of exchange, like goods, words, and women.

By means of successive and rigorous reductions, Lévi-Strauss travels the road of modern philosophy except in the opposite direction, and in order to arrive at diametrically opposite conclusions. In his first move, he reduces the plurality of societies and histories to a dichotomy which encompasses and dissolves them: primitive thought and civilized thought. Immediately, he discovers that this opposition is part of another fundamental opposition: nature and culture. In a third step, he reveals the identity between the latter two things: the products of culture—myths, institutions, language—are not essentially different from natural products, nor do they obey different laws from those which rule their homologues, cells. Everything is living material which changes. Matter itself evaporates: it is an operation, a relation. Culture is a metaphor of the human spirit and this is nothing but a metaphor of the cells and their chemical reactions, which, in turn, are but another metaphor. We come from nature and we return to it. Except that now it is a jungle of symbols: real trees and wild animals, insects and birds, have been transformed into equations. We can now see more clearly what constitutes Lévi-

Strauss's opposition to the dichotomy between history and structure, primitive and civilized thought. It is not that he thinks it wrong, but rather that, however decisive it may be *for us*, it is not really essential. Certainly, the historical event is "powerful—but lifeless": its domain is contingency. Every event is unique and in this sense, it is not structuralism, but history, which can to a certain degree explain it. At the same time, all events are ruled by the structure, that is, by a universal unconscious reason. The latter is identical among savages and among the civilized: we think different things in the same way. Structure is not historical: it is natural, and in it resides the real human *nature*. It is a return to Rousseau, but to a Rousseau who might have passed through the Platonic Academy. For Rousseau, natural man was passional man; for Lévi-Strauss, passions and sensibility are also relations, and do not escape reason and number, the mathematical relations. Human nature, while not an essence or an *idea*, is a concerto, a harmony, a *proportion*.

In a world of symbols, what do symbols symbolize? Not man, for if there is no subject, man is not the being signified or the being signifying. Man is barely a moment in the message which nature sends and receives. Nature, for its part, is not a substance or a thing: it is a message. What does that message say?

The question I raised when I began and which has reappeared time and time again in these pages, returns and turns into the final question: what does thought say, what is the meaning of meaning? Nature is structure, and structure sends forth meanings; therefore, it is not possible to silence the question about meaning. Philosophy, in the guise of semantics, intervenes in a conversation where no one has invited it but which, without it, would lack *meaning*. For a message to be understood it is indispensable for the receiver to know the key used by the sender. Men have the presumption, in the double sense of this word, that they know that key, if only partially. Others had thought that the key didn't exist. The foundation of the formers' pretension consisted in thinking that man was the *receiver* of messages sent him by God, the cosmos, nature, or Idea. The latter asserted that man was the *sender*. Kant weakened the first belief and showed that one area of reality was untouchable, inaccessible. His critique undermined traditional metaphysical systems and strengthened the position of those who favored the second hypothesis. By means of the operation of the dialectic, Hegel transformed the inaccessible "thing in itself" into a concept; Marx took the second step and turned the "concept" into "historical nature"; Engels came to believe that "praxis, especially experimentation and industry" had finished off once and for all the "thing in itself," which he called a "philosophical extravagance." The end of the "thing in itself," proclaimed by Hegel and his materialist disciples, was a subversion of the positions in the ancient dialogue which man and the Cosmos maintain: now the former would be the sender and nature would listen. The unintelligibility of nature was transformed, by the creative negation of the concept and praxis, into historical meaning. Man humanizes the cosmos, that is, he gives it meaning: he turns it into language. The question about the meaning of meaning is answered by Marxism in this way: every meaning is historical. *History dissolves being into meaning.* We could call Lévi-Strauss's response to this assertion a meditation on the ruins of Taxila, or Marxism corrected by Buddhism.

Perhaps the most beautiful chapter of that beautiful book *Tristes Tropiques* is the last one. The thought achieves in those few pages a density and transparency which might make us think of statuettes of rock crystal if it were not for the fact that it is animated by a pulsation which does not recall so much mineral immobility as the vibration of light waves. A geometry of brilliance which takes the fascinating shape of the spiral. It is the periwinkle, symbol of wind and word, a sign of movement among the ancient Mexicans: each step is simultaneously a return to the starting point and an advance toward the unknown. That which we abandon at the beginning awaits us transfigured at the end. Change and identity are metaphors of The Same: it repeats itself and is never the same. The ethnographer returns from the New to the Old World and in the ancient land of Gandhara joins both ends of his explorations together: in the Brazilian jungle he had seen how a society is built; in Taxila he contemplates the remains of a civilization which conceived of itself as a meaning which nullifies itself. In the first case, he was a witness of the birth of meaning; in the second, of its negation. A double return: the ethnologist comes back from societies without history to present-day history; the European intellectual returns to a thought which was born 2500 years ago and discovers that in that beginning the end was already written. Time is also a metaphor and its passage is as illusory as our efforts to halt it: it neither flows nor stops. Our very mortality is illusory: every man who dies assures the survival of the species, each species which becomes extinct confirms the persistence of a movement which rushes tirelessly toward an ever-imminent and always unreachable immobility.

Taxila is not only an assemblage of civilizations but

also of gods: the ancient fertility cults and those of Zoroaster, Apollo, and the Great Goddess, Shiva, and the faceless god of Islam. Among all these divinities, the figure of Buddha, the man who refused to be God and who, because of that decision, refused to be man. He thus conquered, at once, the temptation of eternity and the no less insidious temptation of history. Lévi-Strauss points out the absence of Christian monuments in Taxila. I do not know if he is correct in thinking that Islam prevented the meeting between Buddhism and Christianity, but he is not mistaken when he says that that meeting would have driven off the terrible spell which has driven the West mad: its frantic race in search of power and self-destruction. Buddhism is the connective matter which is missing in the chain of our history. It is the first knot and the last: the knot which, when it comes undone, undoes the entire string. The affirmation of historical meaning culminates inevitably in a negation of meaning: "Between the Marxist critique which liberates man from his first chains, and the Buddhist critique which consummates his liberation, there is no opposition nor contradiction." A double movement which joins the beginning with the end: that which Buddha proposed to us at the beginning of our history is perhaps only realizable at the end of it: only the man free of the burden of historical necessity and of the tyranny of authority will be able to contemplate fearlessly his own nothingness. The history of Western thought and science have been nothing but a series "of supplementary demonstrations of the conclusion from which we would like to escape": the distinction between the meaning and the absence of meaning is illusory.

I said at the outset that Peirce's reply to the question about meaning was circular: the meaning of meaning is to mean. As in the case of Marxism, Lévi-Strauss does not deny or contradict Peirce's answer; he picks it up, and true to the spiral motion, confronts it with itself: sense and non-sense are the same. This assertion is a repetition of the ancient word of the Enlightened One and, at the same time, it is a different word and one which only a twentieth-century man could give voice to. It is the truth of the principle, transfigured by our history and revealed only to us: the meaning is an operation, a relationship. A psycho-chemical combination of stimuli and responses or of impermanent and unsubstantial *dharmas*, the ego does not exist. There exists an "us" and its existence is barely the blink of an eye, a combination of elements which have no existence of their own either. Each man and each society are doomed to "drill through the wall of necessity" and to fulfill the hard task of history, knowing that each movement of liberation encloses them even more in their prison. Is there no way out, is there no *other shore?* The "Golden Age is in ourselves" and it is momentary: that infinitesimal instant in which—whatever our beliefs, our civilization, and the period in which we live—we feel not like an isolated ego, nor like an "us" lost in the labyrinth of the ages but like a part of the whole, a throbbing in the universal respiration—outside of time, outside of history, immersed in the motionless light of a mineral, in the white perfume of a magnolia, in the fleshy and almost black abyss of a poppy, in the look "pregnant with patience, serenity, and mutual forgiveness which we sometimes exchange with a cat." Lévi-Strauss calls those moments: *detachment.* I would add that they are also an *un-knowing:* a dissolution of meaning into being, although we know that being is identical to nothingness.

The West teaches us that being is dissolved into meaning, and the East that meaning is dissolved into something which is neither being nor nonbeing: in a The Same which no language except the language of silence names. For men are made in such a way that silence is also a language for us. The word of Buddha has meaning, though it asserts that nothing has, because it aims in the direction of silence: if we wish to

know what he really said, we ought to question his silence. Now then, the interpretation of what Buddha *did not say* is the axis of the great controversy which has divided schools of Buddhism from the beginning. Tradition tells us that the Enlightened One did not answer ten questions: is the world eternal or not? is the world infinite or not? are body and soul the same or are they different? will Tathagata live on after death or not, or both things, or neither one? Some of those questions could not be answered; others Gautama did not know how to answer; and still others he preferred not to answer. K. N. Jayatilleke translates the interpretations of the schools into modern terms.*
If Buddha did not know the answers he was a skeptic or a simple agnostic; if he preferred to remain silent because to answer them might turn his listeners from the true path, he was a pragmatic reformer; if he was silent because there was no possible response, he was an agnostic rationalist (the questions were beyond the bounds of reason) or a logical positivist (the questions lacked meaning, and therefore, answers). The young Singhalese professor leans toward the last solution. Despite the fact that historical tradition seems to contradict him, his hypothesis seems to me plausible if we

* *Early Buddhist Theory of Knowledge*, London [Allen and Unwin], 1963.

remember the extremely intellectual character of Buddhism, based on a combinatorial theory of the world and of the ego which foreshadows contemporary logic. But this interpretation, not very distant from Lévi-Strauss's position, forgets another possibility: silence, in itself, is an answer. That was the interpretation of the Madhyamaka school, and of Nagarjuna and his disciples. There are two silences: one, after the word, is a knowledge that the only thing worth saying cannot be said. Buddha said everything one can say with words: the errors and achievements of reason, the truth and falsehood of the senses, the resplendance and the void of the instant, the freedom and the slavery of nihilism. The word full of reasons which cancel each other out and which devour each other. But his silence says something different.

The essence of the word is relation, and that is why it is the key, the momentary incarnation of everything which is relative. Every word engenders a word which contradicts it, every word is a relation between negation and affirmation. Relation is to tie together othernesses, it is not the resolution of contradictions. Therefore, language is the realm of dialectic which ceaselessly destroys itself and is reborn only to die. If Buddha's silence were the expression of this relativism, it would not be silence, but word. That is not the way it is: with his silence, movement, operation, dialectic, word, cease. At the same time, it is not the negation of dialectic nor of movement: Buddha's silence is the *resolution* of language. We come from silence and to silence we return: to the word which has ceased to be word. What Buddha's silence says is neither negation nor affirmation. It says *sunyata*: everything is empty because everything is full, the word is not a statement because the only statement is silence. Not nihilism but relativism, which destroys itself and goes beyond itself. Movement does not resolve itself in immobility: it *is* immobility, and immobility is movement. The negation of the world implies a return to the world, asceticism is a return to the senses, samsara is nirvana, reality is the beloved and terrible key to irreality, the instant is not the refutation, but the incarnation, of eternity, the body is not a window on the infinite: it is the infinite itself. Have we noticed that the senses are at the same time senders and receivers of all sense? To reduce the world to meaning is as absurd as reducing it to the senses. The fullness of the senses: there sense fades away so that a moment later it can contemplate the way in which sensation is dispelled. Vibration, waves, signals, and responses: silence. Not the knowledge of the void: an *empty knowledge*. Buddha's silence is not a knowledge but rather something after knowledge: wisdom. An un-knowing. A being loose and thus resolved. Quietude is the dance, and the ascetic's solitude is identical, in the center of the immobile spiral, to the embrace of the loving couples in the sanctuary at Karli. A knowledge that knows nothing and that culminates in a poetics and in an erotics. An instantaneous act, a form that disintegrates, a word that vanishes: the art of dancing above the abyss.

Delhi
17 December 1966

Notes

1. One of the most grotesque consequences of Stalinist obscurantism was the introduction of the pejorative adjective "formalist" into artistic and literary discussions. For years, pseudo-Marxist critics marked with the disreputable stamp of that word many poems, paintings, novels, and musical works. This accusation turned out to be even more idiotic in countries like ours, in which no one knew what the word "formalist" really meant. Somewhat as if the Archbishop of Mexico, hypnotized by a Brahmin from Benares, damned our Protestants not for Christian heresy, but because they committed the errors of Buddha. Among Russian formalists, we find two of the founders of structural linguistics: Nicolai Sergeevich Trubetskoi, and Roman Jakobson. Both of them left the Soviet Union in the 1920's and played a decisive role in the work of the linguistic school of Prague. The former died in 1939, an indirect victim of the Nazis; the latter, also pursued by the brown shirts, took refuge in the United States and today is a professor at Harvard. The history of Russian formalism is intimately tied to that of futurism. Maiakovskii, Khlebnikov, Burliuk, and other poets and painters of the group participated in the linguistic discussions of the formalists.

A close friend of Maiakovskii, the critic Osip Brik, was one of the proponents of the Society for Studies on Poetic Language (Opoias). Maiakovskii was present the night Jakobson read his essay on Khlebnikov and, according to one witness, "he listened intensely to the abstruse reasoning of the young linguist, in which he examined the prosody of the futurists in the light of concepts derived from Edmund Husserl and Ferdinand de Saussure." (Victor Erlich, *Russian Formalism* [2nd rev. ed.; The Hague: Mouton, 1965]).

2. It would be worth while to analyze, from this point of view, the mythology of ancient Mexico. Meso-American religions are an immense cosmic ballet of transformations, a grandiose dance of disguises in which each name is a date and a mask, a bundle of contradictory attributes. For example, Quetzalcóatl. He is a Messiah, a typical mediator. On the historical level he is a mediator between the cultures of the coast of the Gulf of Mexico and those of the high plateau, the great theocracies and the Toltecs, the Náhuatl world and the Maya; on the cosmological level he is between the earth (serpent) and the sky (bird), the air (the mask in the shape of a duck's beak) and the water (periwinkle), the underground world (descent into hell) and the heavenly (the planet Venus); on the magico-moral level he is between sacrifice and self-sacrifice, penitence and excess, continence and indulgence, drunkenness and sobriety. He is a myth of emergence (the origin of man) and a myth of transition; he is the image of

time, the embodiment of movement, its goal and its transfiguration (the self-immolation by fire and his metamorphosis into a planet). An astronomical myth and a culture hero, he is above all a crystallization of the duality, the key to the riddle of the relationship between this and the unity. His name means "precious twin" and his double is Xóolotl. The latter has many names, shapes, and attributes: dog, cripple (like Oedipus), tiger, sexual divinity, amphibious animal (*axólotl*). Naturally we would have to put all these relationships off to one side, to approach the myth with innocent and objective eyes, and after collecting all the variants, place the pertinent mythemes in a chart. On the other hand, the meaning of the figure of Quetzalcóatl will only become intelligible the day it is studied as part of a vaster mythic system which embraces not only Meso-America but also the north of the continent, and probably also South America. The plurality of societies which took up and modified the myth prevents its being studied by means of the historical method. The only adequate one, thus, would be Lévi-Strauss's. For the present, I note something obvious: the story of Quetzalcóatl is in reality a group of stories, a family of myths, or, more precisely, a system. Its theme is mediation. The location of Quetzalcóatl's temple in Tenochtitlán, between those dedicated to Tláloc and to Huitzilopochtli, reveals a sort of triangle in which the figure of Quetzalcóatl is a point of union between two mythical constellations, one associated with the planets and water, and the other an astronomical and warrior one. This duality, as Soustelle has observed, corresponds also to the structure of Aztec society and to the peculiar situation of this people in the context of the cultures of the high plateau: Huitzilopochtli was the Aztec tribal god, while Tláloc represents a much older cult. I will recall, finally, that the Holy Pontiff among the Aztecs bore the name of Quetzalcóatl and that, as Sahagún tells us, "there were two high priests."

3. To see myths as sentences or parts of a discourse made up of all the myths of a civilization is a disconcerting but bracing idea. Applied to literature, for example, it reveals to us a different and perhaps more exact image of what we call tradition. Instead of being a succession of names, works, and tendencies, tradition would become a system of significant relations: a language. Góngora's poetry would not only be something that comes after Garcilaso and before Rubén Darío, but a text in dynamic relation with other texts; we would read Góngora not as an isolated text, but in his context: those works which determine him and those his poetry determines. If we conceive of poetry in the Spanish language more as system than as history, the significance of the works which make it up does not depend so much on chronology nor on our point of view, as on the relations of the texts with each other and of the very movement of the system. The significance of Quevedo is not exhausted in his works, nor in seventeenth-century conceptism; we find the meaning

of his word more fully in some poem of Vallejo's, although, naturally, what the Peruvian poet says is not identical to what Quevedo tried to say. The meaning is transformed without disappearing: each transmutation, as it changes it, extends it. The relation between one work and another is not merely chronological or, rather, that relation is variable and changes chronology endlessly: to *hear* what the poems of Juan Ramón Jiménez's last period say, one must read a fourteenth-century song (e.g., *Aquel árbol que mueve la hoja* . . . by the Admiral Hurtado de Mendoza). Lévi-Strauss's idea invites us to see Spanish literature not as a collection of works, but as one single work. That work is a system, a language in movement, and in relation with other systems: the other European literatures and their American descendents.

4. When this book was finished, the excellent study which M. Louis Dumont has devoted to the castes of India (*Homo hierarchicus*, Paris [Gallimard, 1967]), reached me. The French anthropologist rejects the historical explanation which I have noted, but on the other hand he agrees with me to a certain extent in seeing something like a sort of diametrical opposition between the Hindu social system and that of the modern West: in the former, the element—if in fact we can speak of elements—is not the individual, but rather castes and society, conceived of as a relation, are hierarchical; in the latter, the element is the individual and society is egalitarian. I have devoted a long commentary to M. Dumont's ideas in *Corriente*

alterna [México: Siglo XXI] (1967). In the same book I deal at greater length with the theme of the opposition between communication and meditation, drunkenness and drugs. Here I will only say that the two most significant images of our tradition are the Platonic Banquet and the last Supper of Christ. Both are symbols of communication and even of communion; in both, wine occupies a central place. The East, on the other hand, has exalted above all the hermit: Gautama the recluse, the yogi in the shadow of the banyan tree or in the solitude of a cave. Now then, alcoholism is an exaggeration of communication; the taking of drugs, its negation. The former is part of the tradition of the Banquet (the philosophical dialogue), and communion (the mystery of the Eucharist); the latter, part of the tradition of solitary contemplation. In Western countries, the authorities until recently used to be concerned about the social dangers of alcoholism; today they are beginning to be alarmed by the ever-widening use of hallucinogens. In the first case, we have to deal with an *abuse*; in the case of drugs, with a *dissidence*. Isn't this a symptom of a change of values in the West, especially in the most advanced and prosperous nation: the United States?

5. Lévi-Strauss's conception recalls, on the one hand, Hume, and on the other, Buddha. The similarity with Buddhism is extraordinary: "In Buddhism there is not percipient apart from perception, no conscious subject behind consciousness. . . . The term *subject* must be

understood to mean not the self-same permanent conscious subject but merely a transitory state of consciousness. . . . The object of Abhidhamma is to show that there is not soul or ego apart from the states of consciousness; but that each seemingly simple state is in reality a highly complex compound, constantly changing and giving rise to new combinations" [tr. note: in English in the original]. (S. Z. Aung, in his Introduction to *Abhidhammattha-Sangha*, Pali Text Society, 1963.) Despite the similarity between Buddhist thought and Lévi-Strauss's the latter does not accept either ascetic renunciation (it strikes him as egoistical), nor even less, that unspeakable and undefinable (except in negative terms) reality which we call Nirvana. He must feel even farther, I suppose, from the points of view of Mahayana Buddhism. Surely, the idea that all the elements (dharmas) are interdependent is not unique to his conception, and neither is seeing in them simple *names* empty of substance; on the contrary, to deduce from this relativism an absolute which is to a certain extent ineffable, must cause him to feel a certain intellectual repugnance. The paradox of Buddhism does not lie in its being a religious philosophy but in its being a philosophical religion: it reduces reality to a flow of signs and names, but asserts that wisdom and sanctity (one and the same thing) reside in the disappearance of the signs. "The signs of the Tathagata," says the sutra Vagrakkhedika, "are the non-signs." I will say finally that the similarity between Buddhism and Lévi-Strauss's thought is not accidental: it is one more proof that the West, by its own means, and by the very logic of its history, is now arriving at conclusions fundamentally identical to those Buddha and his disciples had arrived at. Human thought is one, and we owe it to Lévi-Strauss—among many other things—to have demonstrated that the reason of the primitive or of the Oriental is no less rigorous than our own.

Bibliographical Note

SOME MAJOR WORKS OF
CLAUDE LÉVI-STRAUSS

Anthropologie structurale, Paris: Plon, 1958; in English: *Structural Anthropology*, trans. Claire Jacobson and Brooke Grundfest Schoepf, New York: Basic Books, 1963, and Garden City, N.Y.: Anchor Books, 1967.

Le Cru et le cuit; Mythologiques, I, Paris: Plon, 1964; in English: *The Raw and the Cooked: Introduction to a Science of Mythology, I*, trans. John and Doreen Weightman, New York: Harper and Row, 1969.

Leçon inaugurale, Paris: Collège de France, 1960; in English: *The Scope of Anthropology*, trans. Sherry Ortner Paul and Robert A. Paul, London: Cape, 1967.

La Pensée sauvage, Paris: Plon, 1962; in English: *The Savage Mind*, Chicago: University of Chicago Press, 1966.

Les Structures élémentaires de la parenté, Paris: Presses Universitaires de France, 1949; in English: *The Elementary Structures of Kinship*, rev. ed., trans. James Harle Bell, John Richard von Sturmer, and Rodney Needham, ed., Boston: Beacon Press, 1969.

153

Le Totémisme aujourd'hui, Paris: Presses Universitaires de France, 1962; in English: *Totemism*, trans. Rodney Needham, Boston: Beacon Press, 1963.

Tristes Tropiques, Paris: Plon, 1955; in English: trans. John Russell, New York: Criterion Books, 1961, and New York: Atheneum, 1967.

Index

Claude Lévi-Strauss: An Introduction

Designed by R. E. Rosenbaum.
Composed by Vail-Ballou Press, Inc.,
in 11 point linotype Electra, 4 points leaded,
with display lines in monotype Deepdene.
Printed from letterpress plates by Vail-Ballou Press, Inc.,
on Warren's No. 66 Text, 60 pound basis,
with the Cornell University Press watermark.
Bound by Vail-Ballou Press, Inc.,
in Joanna Arrestox B cloth
and stamped in imitation gold foil.